LIVE YOUR BEST LIFE

Essays on authenticity, confidence
& resilience

Ben Wardle

benwardle.org

CONTENTS

Title Page   1

INTRODUCTION   7

1. YOU DESERVE TO BE HAPPY   12

2. TURN YOUR DREAMS INTO YOUR REALITY   18

3. STOP APOLOGISING FOR WHO YOU ARE   27

4. KNOW YOUR VALUES & PRINCIPLES   33

5. MAKE LOVE YOUR SUPREME GUIDING LIGHT   41

6. PURSUE YOUR TRUE PASSIONS   45

7. PERSEVERANCE IS KEY   50

8. ADVERSITY FORGES CHARACTER   56

9. ASPIRE NOT TO HAVE MORE BUT TO BE MORE   63

10. EMBRACE YOUR EMOTIONS   70

11. WHAT OTHER PEOPLE THINK OF YOU IS NONE OF   77
YOUR BUSINESS

12. IF YOU WOULDN'T TAKE THEIR ADVICE, DON'T   81
LISTEN TO THEIR CRITICISM

13. ALWAYS REMEMBER THAT YOU ARE ENOUGH   86

14. DON'T LET ANYBODY INTIMIDATE YOU   91

15. YOUR ATTITUDE IS EVERYTHING   98

16. STOP UNDERESTIMATING YOURSELF!   105

17. STAND UP FOR YOURSELF   109

18. STOP HOLDING BACK   116

19. CHALLENGE YOUR IRRATIONAL BELIEFS   121

20. MAKE FULFIlMENT YOUR FOCUS   130

21. STOP MAKING EXCUSES   134

22. MAKE INNER PEACE YOUR PRIORITY   138

23. MAKE CONENCTION YOUR CURRENCY   147

24. CULTIVATE MEANINGFUL RELATIONSHIPS   152

25. MOVE BEYOND FEAR   159

26. THE CULTIVATION OF CHARACTER   163

27. KNOW THAT CHANGE IS THE ONLY CONSTANT IN LIFE   168

28. KNOW YOURSELF   173

29. INVEST IN YOURSELF   177

30. THE IMPORTANCE OF SELF LOVE   183

     187

31. GRATITUDE LEADS TO GREATNESS

32. GET YOUR PRIORITIES RIGHT   193

33. DON'T THINK ABOUT IT, JUST DO IT   197

34. STRIVE TO BE INTERESTED, NOT INTERESTING   200

35. ALWAYS ACT LIKE YOU ARE LIKED   205

36. THE 'MEET & GREET MINDSET'   210

37. HOW TO TALK TO ANYBODY   219

38. BEYOND BELIEF: FILLING THE RELIGIONLESS VOID   226

39. KNOWLEDGE IS POWER   231

40. LET'S GET PHILOSOPHICAL!   236

41. NEVER GET BITTER, ALWAYS GET BETTER   246

42. MAKE PEACE WITH YOUR PAST   251

43. LET GO OF GRUDGES   256

44. TURN IMPULSIVE REACTIONS INTO INTELLIGENT   263
RESPONSES

45. HOW TO HANDLE THE HATERS   267

46. USE SOCIAL MEDIA RESPONSIBLY   277

47. DON'T FEAR DIFFICULT CONVERSATIONS   283

48. CELEBRATE LIFE'S SIMPLE PLEASURES   290

49. TRY A NEW PERSPECTIVE!   294

50. DON'T TAKE YOURSELF TOO SERIOUSLY   299

51. ENJOY EVERYTHING IN MODERATION   305

52. CELEBRATE EVERY ACHIEVEMENT   309

53. WHATEVER HAPPENS IN LIFE, YOU CAN HANDLE   315
IT

AFTERWORD   321

INTRODUCTION

ARE YOU READY TO START LIVING YOUR BEST LIFE?

"The secret of getting ahead is getting started" (Popular Aphorism)

ARE YOU READY TO START LIVING YOUR BEST LIFE? ARE YOU READY TO START SEIZING EACH DAY AS AN OTHER PRECIOUS OPPORTUNITY TO BECOME THE VERY BEST VERSION OF YOURSELF?

Our lives are so precious. We only get one shot at our time here on earth – **life is not a dress rehearsal!** This is your one lifetime, and you never know which day is going to be your last.

With this in mind, I passionately believe that we must make the most of every single opportunity that we have here on this planet! Every single person – starting with you – deserves to live a genuinely happy and deeply fulfilling life. That's right, **YOU DESERVE TO BE HAPPY! And *every* single day of your life deserves to be lived to the absolute full!** Instead of holding back and being controlled by your fears, you deserve to live fearlessly as the best version of yourself! And guess what? YOU CAN!

You are the master of your own destiny. You are completely and utterly in charge of your own life. So don't you dare start outsourcing responsibility or giving other people power over your life!

It is 100% within your power to start living your best life!

Happiness is not something that is just handed to us on a plate. Success is not some kind of overnight miracle. We don't just end up feeling fulfilled as a result of having a bit of good luck!

You are the author of your whole entire life, and the direction of your whole entire life is completely down to you.

Let me tell you something: **you have a limitless potential and this lifetime presents you with the most extraordinary opportunity to fulfill it.**

That is not to say that your life is going to be plain-sailing.

Nobody promised you that life was going to be easy! But what I can promise you is this: **whatever happens in your life, you can handle it.**

Whatever challenges you are confronted with, you can overcome them.

Life, wrote the philosopher Kierkegaard, is not a problem to be solved but a reality to be experienced.

And so from this very moment, you need to start realising your strength, knowing your worth & allowing yourself to enjoy your extraordinary journey through this phenomenon that we call life!

Each of the essays in this collection is focused on my core belief that you can 'live your best life' by becoming 'the very best version of yourself'.

Each essay is grounded in my fundamental belief that every

single human being deserves to live a genuinely happy and deeply fulfilling life.

As you'll discover as you read the essays in this book, **I strongly believe that the purpose of life is to fulfil your potential as a human being by becoming the very best version of yourself.**

Life is all about enjoying every single step of the journey and knowing that whatever happens, you can handle it.

So, what should you expect from this little collection of essays? Well, you'll find essays on everything from **making peace with your past** to **confidently handling the haters**. You'll read about **making love your guiding light** and knowing that **whatever happens in life, you can handle it**. There are reflections on **cultivating meaningful relationships** and tips on **challenging the irrational beliefs that hold you back from living your life to the full.**

I hope that the essays in this collection are able to offer you real inspiration and empowerment as you go about your daily life.

I hope that each essay provides you with an opportunity to reflect on where you're at in life, and that each page you read offers you a chance to consider how you might make your existence that little bit more enjoyable and fulfiling.

As well as finding inspirational quotes from some of the greatest thinkers in philosophy and psychology, you'll also find my lists of 'top tips' for dealing with the different trials and tribulations that we all face in everyday life!

Each of the essays that follow has been lovingly written from the heart, and each features my personal life experiences, as well as wisdom I have learned from some of the greatest philosophers to have ever-lived!

◆ ◆ ◆

Ultimately, I believe that **life is a never-ending journey of personal growth and self development.** This is an idea first explored by the Ancient Greek philosophers over 2,500 years ago, and I hope to be able to bring their ideas about flourishing through life for you today.

When it comes to finding happiness, I passionately believe that **the process is so much more important than the final product**.

We are all students attending the 'School of Life', and **each day is another opportunity for personal growth and development**. Every day presents us with an opportunity to **learn from our mistakes, grow through adversity, and to overcome our biggest fears.**

In other words, each day is another precious opportunity to live your very best life by becoming the very best version of yourself.

So stop struggling against life and start appreciating every opportunity that the universe hands to you! Stop fearing failure and start recognising your unconditional worth as a human being!

I truly hope that the essays in this collection will give you the encouragement and motivation to keep putting yourself out there and to keep doing more of the things that make you genuinely happy.

You have just one life, and you deserve to live every single day of it to the absolute full!

May you seize every opportunity to take on new challenges and fulfil your potential as a human being.

Remember, **you were born not just to survive... but to THRIVE!** It's time to know your worth, face your fears...and

LIVE YOUR BEST LIFE!

1.YOU DESERVE TO BE HAPPY

"The very purpose of our life is to seek happiness. That is clear. We all are seeking something better in life. The very motion of our life is towards happiness..." (His Holiness the Dalai Lama XIV)

Ever since our evolutionary ancestors developed the capacity for conscious thought and reflection, mankind has grappled with one fundamental question - what is the purpose of our lives?

Philosophers, psychologists and everyday human beings alike have all spent thousands of years grappling with the age-old predicament - what is the meaning of our human lives?

It is my passionate belief that the fundamental purpose of our existence on this planet is to become a genuinely happy, fulfilled and purpose-driven human being.

That's right, **the purpose of your life is to be happy**. Or, as His Holiness the Dalai Lama puts it, **'the *very motion* of our life is towards happiness'**.

It was the Ancient Greek philosopher Aristotle who first spoke about happiness as the purpose of our human lives. He wrote over 2,500 years ago that **'happiness, then, is the best, noblest and most pleasant thing in the world'**. Indeed, in his book of Nicomachean Ethics, Aristotle famously describes happiness as the **'meaning and purpose of human life, the whole aim and end of human existence'**.

More recently, the 18th century utilitarian philosopher Jeremy Bentham wrote that **'the greatest happiness of the greatest number is the foundation of morals and legislations'**. In the same century, John Stuart Mill wrote that every individual should dedicate their lives to the maximisation of happiness and the minimisation of harm. Each individual, he believed, should have the absolute freedom to do whatever made them genuinely happy in life, as long as this did not involve causing harm to anybody else.

As Mill wrote in his 1859 text 'On Liberty', the **'only purpose for which power can be rightfully exercised over any member of a civilised society...is to prevent harm to others'**. Mill believed very strongly tha**t 'Over your own body and mind, you are sovereign'**. This concept of individual autonomy forms the foundation for my understanding of happiness - **in order to become a genuinely happy human being, I strongly believe that you need to live a fearlessly authentic and absolutely autonomous life.**

Here's what I want you to know: **As a free-thinking individual, you are the master of your own destiny. As an autonomous human being, you have the absolute freedom to do whatever brings you genuine happiness and fulfilment in life.** It is my passionate belief that every individual deserves the freedom to flourish and that every individual should be given the opportunity to live their best possible life as an authentic and autonomous human being.

When it comes to understanding happiness, we need to realise that quality is so much more important than quantity. **Happiness is not the quantity of pleasure we experience but the quality of our lives as a whole.** It is much more than physical pleasure or sensual indulgence - happiness is all about living a genuinely meaningful and deeply fulfilling life.

As John Stuart Mill wrote, **'it is better to be Socrates [the Ancient Greek philosopher] dissatisfied than a pig satisfied'** - the quality of your happiness matters so much more than the quantity. Mill differentiated between 'higher' and 'lower' pleasures. He believed that higher pleasures (intellectual pursuits such as reading, debating or education) were much more desirable than lower pleasures (pleasures of the flesh such as food, drink, drugs and sex). Unlike higher pleasures, which are uniquely human, the lower pleasures are also devoured and enjoyed by animals. In order to become the best version of yourself as a human being, **it is essential that you pursue the higher pleasures and avoid the temptations of the lower pleasures.**

Therefore, when we talk about human happiness as a worthy and noble pursuit, we are not talking about chasing a temporary feeling of pleasure or gratification (which is, of course, what the lower pleasures will provide). We are talking about something much deeper and much more meaningful - **true happiness is achieved by fulfilling your potential and flourishing as an individual.** This true happiness can only ever be attained through the pursuit and cultivation of the higher pleasures in life, which are only accessible to intelligent and autonomous human beings.

His Holiness the Dalai Lama puts it like this:

"When we speak of experiencing happiness, we need to know that there are actually two different kinds. The first is the enjoyment of pleasure through our senses. Here, sex, is one such experience. But we can also experience happiness at a deeper level through our mind, such as love, compassion and generosity. What characterizes happiness at this deeper level is the sense of fulfillment that you experience. Whilst the joy of the senses is brief, the joy at this deeper level is much

longer lasting. It is true joy".

Every single one of us has a deep-rooted desire to live a happy and fulfilling life. And here's the truth – **it is completely within your power to create this happy and fulfilling life for yourself!**

So, what are the best sources of this genuine happiness and fulfilment in our lives? How can we cultivate this contentment and satisfaction in our own existence?

This is a question that has kept countless philosophers up all night for quite literally 2,500 years...and there is still no universally agreed solution! The Stoics, for example, believed that happiness came from controlling your desires and disciplining your mind. The Christians, on the other hand, believed that happiness came from becoming a follower of Jesus Christ and dedicating your life to God. Meanwhile, the Aristotelians believed that happiness came from fulfilling your potential and becoming the best version of yourself.

It is my passionate belief – and it is the central message of this book – that this Aristotelian approach to happiness is the most successful and rewarding. This approach finds its origins in the philosophy of Aristotle, who lived in Ancient Athens over 2,500 years ago. Aristotle believed that **happiness was the product of fulfilling your potential as a human being**. He understood happiness as being the achievement of *'eudaimonia'*, which roughly translates into modern English as *'to flourish'*. **Aristotle was very clear: the purpose of human life - and the source of all human happiness - is to fulfil your potential as an individual and to flourish through each day.**

Happiness in life is all about living your life with a real sense

of purpose. We flourish as human beings when we connect with our values and fulfill our potential as intelligent and autonomous individuals.

It's important to realise that the achievement of 'flourishing' and 'happiness' is subjective to each and every single individual. By this, I mean that **each of us is a unique agent with a unique purpose and potential to fulfill.**

Subsequently, there is no singular definition of happiness because happiness depends on each individual discovering and fulfilling their own unique potential. For example, one person may feel that their purpose in life is to become a parent, whilst another may believe they will thrive in life by becoming a teacher. Someone else may believe that will find fulfilment through excelling in a particular sport. Each individual is different and deserves an equal opportunity to become the very best version of themselves.

John Stuart Mill wrote back in 1859 that **"In proportion to the development of his individuality, each person becomes more valuable to himself, and is, therefore, capable of being more valuable to others"**. He adds that when a man is able to cultivate individuality and fulfill his potential, "there is a greater fullness of life about his own existence". According to Mill, **"It is only [this] cultivation of individuality which produces, or can produce, well-developed human beings"**.

Here's what you need to know: **you are not just here to conform and fit in! You are here to pursue your passions, fulfill your purpose - and live an unashamedly authentic life!** *You are here, in short, to live a genuinely happy and deeply fulfilling life!*

When it comes to finding true happiness in your life, **nothing matters more than discovering your authentic purpose and striving to fulfill your unique potential as a human being.**

The journey to fulfilling your potential as a human being starts with asking yourself three essential questions: what does 'living your best life' look like to me? What people, places, activities, careers, and lifestyles excite and invigorate me the most? What would it look like for me to be living as the 'best possible version of myself?'

I strongly believe that we find happiness and become the best version of ourselves when we **connect with three key things in life:**

- Our purpose, which includes our core values in life.

- Other people, through forming meaningful connections and relationships.

- The present moment, the only place we can find inner peace and fully connect with the universe.

 We need a strong sense of purpose, secure relationships with other human beings, and a stable grounding in the present moment in order to achieve happiness. We need to become **fearlessly authentic** and become stoically prepared to **work relentlessly hard at turning all of our dreams into our brand-new reality.**

Remember, happiness is not just a temporary feeling of pleasure but is instead the **deep sense of purpose that is achieved through fulfilling your potential as an individual!** Make the pursuit of this genuine happiness and fulfilment your new number one priority in life!

Remember this: **You deserve to be happy.** You deserve to fulfil your potential. And you deserve to be living your best life!

Most importantly, remember that you have already got within you ALL of the resources that you're ever going to need in order to truly thrive through life. So what are you waiting for? Unlock your potential, discover your life's purpose...and start living your best life!

2. TURN YOUR DREAMS INTO YOUR REALITY

"First tell yourself what kind of person you want to be, then do what you have to do. For in nearly every pursuit we see this to be the case. Those in athletic pursuit first choose the sport they want and then do that work" (Epictetus)

As autonomous human beings, we have an extraordinary amount of responsibility for the shape and direction of our lives. What you do and who you become in this world is **completely and utterly down to you**. More specifically, it is down to the **decisions** that you make.

The 16th century philosopher John Locke famously believed that each man is born 'tabula rasa', which in modern english translates as 'a blank slate'. This means that you are born with the freedom and power to choose the entire direction of your whole life. There is no divine plan for what is going to happen in your life - it is all completely and utterly down to you. As I always say, you are the master of your own destiny! You can therefore achieve whatever you want in this lifetime - as long as you stay focused on your goals and work hard to turn your biggest dreams into your brand-new reality!

I passionately believe that in order to get what you want in

life, you need to firstly know what it is that you actually want. An archer is unlikely to hit a target they did not aim for. It's hard for a footballer to score a goal when they are not intentionally kicking the ball towards the net.

As Jesus teaches in the New Testament: **"Ask and it will be given to you; seek and you will find; know and the door will be opened to you. For everyone who asks receives; the one who seeks finds; and to the one who knocks, the door will be opened"** (Matthew 7:7).

You need to dream big and then work tirelessly hard to turn your biggest dreams into your brand-new reality! As Denis Waitley and Reni L Witt write, your **'dreams are powerful reflections of your actual growth potential'**. And as Peter Daniels says, **'Dreaming illustrates your hidden capacities and your unawakened ability'**.

Just dreaming about *what* you want in life is not sufficient. When you want to achieve something, you cannot just *aspire* to achieve it – **you have got to take the effective action that will make it happen!** As J F Kennedy once said, **'things do not happen; things are made to happen'**.

You need to realise that you are the master of your own destiny and the author of your entire future. <u>You therefore have the capability to turn all of your dreams into your brand-new reality.</u>

All that is required is a commitment to hard work and perseverance. **With hard work and perseverance, I passionately believe that absolutely anything is possible.** Turning your dreams into your reality simply depends on making a commitment to becoming the very best version of yourself in every situation that you face.

Turning your dreams into your reality is actually a lot more straightforward than you might have thought. I've discovered that there are only two simple steps that you need to take in order to start living your best life and become the best very version of yourself – yes, just two! So what are they?

- To tell yourself what kind of person you want to be

- To do what you have to do in order to become that person

Look, it's not rocket science...unless you want to become an astronaut, of course! (As you can see, my purpose in life was clearly to become an award-winning comedian!!) In order to fulfill your potential and become the person that you want to be, **you need to be anchored by a strong sense of purpose and be driven by a real passion for hard work.**

In other words, you need to **get passionate about fulfilling your potential!** Change and transformation do not just happen overnight; you can't just sit there on your sofa *wishing* that you had a better life. Lord Alan Sugar did not make his billions by lying in bed and just hoping that when he woke up, everything in his life would suddenly be wonderful. If you want to fulfill your potential and experience real success in life, **you need to get out there and start putting blood, sweat, and tears into making a success of your existence!**

<u>You need to get serious about dreaming big and working hard to turn all of your dreams into your new reality!</u>

The truth of the matter is this: **nothing changes until you do!** Let me repeat that for you once more - *nothing changes until you do.* I just love that quote! It's all very well to have dreams and aspirations about how you would like your life to look, but you have got to realise that they will never be more than figments of your imagination unless you **commit to taking the effective action that will bring about real transformation!**

We are all masters of our own destiny. You have within you all the resources necessary to become the best version of yourself. As far as I can see, **there is absolutely no reason that you cannot fulfil your potential in life.** You have the drive, determination, ambition, and resilience required to transform your life! **You have unlimited potential within your own very soul!**

The journey to living your best life all starts with taking accountability for yourself. According to Hal Elrod, virtually **'all highly successful people embrace a high degree of accountability'.** This gives them **'the leverage they need to take action and create results...even when they don't feel like it'.** If we want to be successful in our lives, we need to start taking full accountability for who we are. **It's time to stop outsourcing responsibility for your life and finally become the master of your own destiny!**

So what on earth are you waiting for? Why are you sitting around wishing things could be better when you could actually be getting busy? Becoming the best version of yourself all starts with **taking accountability for your life and making a commitment to start turning all your dreams into your brand-new reality!**

Remember, **success in life starts with you!** Every single one of your dreams and ambitions can be achieved when you start to **believe in your potential and realise the importance of hard work**! This is the golden rule: **If you can dream it, you can achieve it!**

The only thing standing in-between you and success is...YOU! More specifically, **the only thing that is holding you back from living your best ever life is the self-limiting beliefs inside your own head**. I'm talking about those voices that are always telling you that you're not good enough or that it's never going to work out.

In order to enjoy the success that you deserve in this world, you need to **stop listening to those self-limiting beliefs in your head and start believing in your potential instead.**

In order to live our best lives, we need to realise that the only barrier to success is these self-limiting beliefs inside our own minds. **So Stop listening to those voices telling you that it will be too much hard work or that your journey to success will take too much effort. <u>You need to ignore them!</u>** Instead, start working harder than ever before at turning your dreams into your brand-new reality!

The amount of people going through life with unmet potential is one of the greatest scandals of the 21st century! **Your life is a precious gift, and it should be fearlessly lived to the absolute full.** That means silencing those self-limiting beliefs and fearlessly stepping outside of your comfort zone!

Here's what you need to do: **Become the change you want to see in your life**! Yes, it's really that simple! If you want to live a better life than ever before, all you have to do is _become_ the person that you really want to be! Stop dreaming about it and stop wishing that transformation could happen - **<u>get out there and start putting in the hard work!</u>**

 It's time to start realising your potential and wake up to the fact that **you are capable of achieving all of your dreams in life...and more!**

In my own life, I strive to live every single day to the full by turning my biggest dreams into my reality. For years, I had dreamed of living in London and, at the age of 17 , made the decision to study theology at a top London university! Of course, entry into this university was not going to be handed to me on a plate - I needed to worked ridiculously hard in order to secure the A Levels required to get onto the course! After two years of long hours and thousands of pages worth of reading, it's safe to say all that hard work paid off! I had needed ABB to get onto the course - I ended up coming out with A*A*A (and that A was just 4 marks off an A*, i'll have you know!) I was utterly delighted that all of my hard work and perserverance had paid off - I was now able to turn my dreams into my new reality!

And so in September 2018, aged just 18, I moved down to the Big City from my small hometown in North West England.

At first, I was absolutely terrified and felt utterly over-whelmed by the idea of having to find my way around this enormous city. But I was determined to make a success of the experience and live my very best London life! So I immedi-ately got to work turning my time in London into a success! I have never been afraid of hard work and was determined to work harder than ever before in order to make a triumph of my time in the capital! I knew I needed to become fearless about putting myself out there - if I didn't go out there and get what I wanted, nobody was going to come along and just hand it to me! And so, on my very first weekend in London, I went out and got a job at Europe's biggest LGBT+ nightclub!

 The nightclub is located at the bottom of the Stand, just off Trafalgar Square, and I remember walking down from Em-bankment tube station and thinking 'what the hell am I doing right now?!?!' But I kept my Positive Mindset fixed firmly in my mind - and I got the job! That weekend, I did my first Sat-urday night shift, working from 10pm (when I would usually be tucked up in bed listening to the news on Radio 4) all the way through to 5am (when I would usually be waking up for my morning session of meditation). It was the most incred-ible experience; little 18 year-old-me was excitedly working at the epicentre of London nightlife, in the very centre of the city, and in a club filled with thousands of LGBT+ people.

And whilst working these Saturday nights (from 10pm until 5am, remember!) at the heart of London's thriving gay scene,

I also threw myself into my university course. I even managed to quickly master the London Underground. I became an expert at navigating the Night Tube after finishing at work and surviving on the Central Line during the 7.30am morning rush hour!

Soon, I felt like I could call London home - I knew exactly where I was going (most of the time) and it felt like I was living somewhere that I belonged. My big personality felt perfectly at home in this big city - I loved being so busy and I loved the fast-paced nature of every single day! There was always something to do, somewhere to be and so many people around! I had visualised the life that I had dreamed of living, and had then put in the hard work to turn that dream into my reality!

I had always known that from the moment that I arrived down in London, everything was going to be totally down to me. I was not attending a campus university or continuing my studies at home - living in London would be completely different to living or studying absolutely anywhere else in the world! This is certainly what attracted me to the city in the first place, but it was also what made me most nervous about the experience as well! After all, I was 240 kilometres away from home in the middle of a city populated by 9 million people!

If I wanted to get to university, I had to take on the Central Line - at rush hour! - and quite literally fight my way off the carriage at Holborn. If I wanted food to eat that evening, I had to make my way around the supermarkets of Stratford (Lidl, Sainsburys, Iceland and Waitrose became firm favourites) and if I wanted to actually afford that food, I had to get myself a job and work tirelessly hard every single day of the week.

On a Sunday morning, after getting in from work at 6am, I would pull myself out of bed five hours later and get on with my university essays. On a weekday morning, I would jump out of bed at 6am and prepare myself for another day of rush hour tube journeys, Café Nero coffee dates, Wetherspoons lunches and – of course – university lectures! As I raced my way around London, I was totally outside of my comfort zone...and I was totally loving every single second of it!

I quickly realised that it was totally was down to me whether I thrived in London or became totally overwhelmed by the whole experience. I realised that I had a very clear choice: I could hide away in my bedroom feeling scared of this big city and all these busy people...or I could fearlessly put myself out there and take this city by storm! Thank God that I chose the latter and decided to totally throw myself into London life!

Since making that move down to London, I have never looked back. It was the best decision that I ever made. My life has completely been transformed - I feel like a whole new person who has discovered this most extraordinary self-confidence and resilience! It makes me so proud to think that I have been able to turn my biggest dreams into my new reality through the power of hard work and determination!

I hope that sharing my personal story of moving to London really exemplifies my point that **living your best life starts with you**. It's clear to me that nothing changes in your life until you do, and in order to start fulfiling your potential, you need to start living *fearlessly!*

You need to get serious about putting yourself out there and working hard to turn all of your dreams into your new reality!

Remember that **the only person who can make this transformation happen in your life is you**. You are the captain of your ship and the author of your next chapter!

It is not enough to wish that you had more confidence or to

wish that you achieved more in your life. Thinking about it doesn't change it! The reality is this: **In order to turn your dreams into your reality and become the best version of yourself, you need to take ACTION**. Right here and right now.

What are you most scared of? What is it that's holding you back? Do you want to spend the rest of your whole life in your comfort zone – it may feel safe now, but when you look back in years to come will you not regret not seizing every opportunity to live your best possible life? As I always say, **take control of your life!** Seize the day, step outside of your comfort zone, and start working harder than ever before to turn your dreams into your reality!

Starting today, **commit yourself to becoming the person you want to be in life.** Tell yourself what kind of person you want to be, and then do what you have to do to become that person!

As Samuel Johnson once remarked, **'life affords no higher pleasure than that of surmounting difficulties, passing from one step of success to another, forming new wishes and seeing them granted'.**

Don't just dream about it – make it happen! Believe that you've got what it takes! **Life is tough...but you are tougher!** And so it's about time that you started living your very best life.

Napoleon Hill once said this: **"There is a difference between wishing for a thing and being ready to receive it. No one is ready for a thing until they believe they can acquire it. Before anything can come to us, we have to envision it and believe that it is ours".**

Remember that turning your dreams into your new reality all begins with one thing alone– **YOU!** So roll up your sleeves, stop listening to those self-limiting beliefs in your head...and **fearlessly commit to living your very best life.**

3. STOP APOLOGISING FOR WHO YOU ARE

"As long as you are not causing harm, you should be free to do whatever brings you genuine happiness and fulfilment in life" (Ben Wardle)

If there's one thing that makes my makes my heart break and my blood boil in equal measure, it is seeing people feel like they have to apologise for who they authentically are. Because of the utterly irrelevant and uninvited opinions of other people, so many of us feel like we have to go through life apologising for our appearance or personal identity. *This is an absolute scandal!*

A deep fear of other people's opinions, criticisms and judgements leads to so many people limiting their self-expression as human beings.

So many of us stop ourselves from wearing certain outfits, for example, because we are so scared about what people in the street might say. We try to change or 'tone down' certain aspects of our personality because we are so anxious about what other people - perhaps in the playground or in the workplace - will think about us. We are paralysed by a fear of being picked on and we are desperate to avoid being criticised by others.

As a result of our fears about being rejected and ridiculed, we make a habit of apologising to people for who we are. I have quite literally lost track of the number of times I have heard myself apologising for my personality. Over the years, I must have started hundreds of sentences with the words 'I know that I'm probably too much for you...' or 'I'm sorry that my personality is so flamboyant but...'

After a childhood spent being picked on for being 'gay', 'so over-the-top', 'dramatic' and 'acting like a girl', I have always felt like I need to apologise for the fact some people clearly have a problem with my personality. I always wanted to get my apology in before someone had the chance to start picking apart my personality and brutally assassinating my character.

Now that I am so much more confident in my own skin, I can finally see that this was completely and utterly wrong! Why on earth should you ever feel ashamed of being the best version of yourself? Why on earth should you ever apologise for doing the things that make you genuinely happy?

The truth is this: **as long as you are not causing harm to anybody else, you are free to do absolutely whatever you want and you are free to express yourself in whatever way makes you genuinely happy.**

And so I no longer apologise for having an 'over-the-top' or 'outgoing' personality! I see it like this: **I am not causing anybody any kind of harm whatsoever, and so there is no reason for me to ever apologise for being who I authentically am!**

Of course, that doesn't mean that everybody has to like me, but it does mean that I don't have to apologise to them if they don't! As you'll find out later in this book, I passionately believe that 'what other people think about you is none of your business'. *As long as you aren't causing anybody else any harm, then you shouldn't worry for one second about what other people might think about you!* If they can't cope with your fabulousness, then I'm sorry but that is their problem and not yours!

◆ ◆ ◆

As we read in the New Testament: **"Do not judge, or you too will be judged. For in the same way as you judge others, you will be judged, and with the same measure you use, it will be measured to you"** (Matthew 7:1). People have absolutely no right or reason to start judging your appearance, interests or personality - **as long as you are not causing anybody any harm, you do not have to answer to anybody!**

Back in the 19th century, the liberal philosopher John Stuart Mill encapsulated this idea in his 'non-harm principle'. According to Mill's principle, **every human being is free to do whatever they please as long as they are not causing harm to anybody else.** People have absolutely no right to interfere with the choices that you make in your day-to-day existence! He writes in 'On Liberty', first published in 1859, that "the only purpose for which power can be rightfully exercised over any member of a civilised community, against his will, is to prevent harm to others".

Put simply, **you should be free to do whatever you like in life as long as you are not causing harm to other people.**

You - just as much as anybody else - have a fundamental right to live your life free from persecution, abuse, exploitation, manipulation, attack, bullying or any other kind of intentionally caused harm. Anyone who commits what Mill described as 'acts injurious to others' (anything that caused harm to other people – either directly or indirectly) must face moral reprobation and – in the gravest of cases – punishment. This means that as long as you are not causing harm to anybody else, **you should be free to live your best life and do more of the things that make you genuinely happy.** *And you should never feel ashamed, embarrassed, anxious, or apologetic about doing so.*

According to Mill, **the secret to finding true happiness in life**

is escaping from the prison of public opinion and choosing to start living life on your own terms. Nothing is more important than choosing to take control of your life as an autonomous individual! And that begins with refusing to apologise for who you authentically are!

It is truly heart-breaking to see just how many people spend their whole lives feeling terrified of being mocked, labelled, or singled out. This was the way that I lived my life for so many years! To say that I was absolutely terrified of people's nasty comments or rejection is an understatement! I was absolutely paralysed by a terror of being told that someone didn't like me.

As a result of this desperation for acceptance and approval, so many people go through their lives seeking to suppress their true selves and trying to change their whole identity. Instead of taking control of their lives, these people try to conform and live their lives avoiding the criticism of others. They try and become someone who they think that **other** people will approve of, failing to realise that all this will lead to is a life of sadness, frustration, fear and alienation.

Of course, it does always feel safer to be a sheep and to fit in. It is a lot safer to conform rather take the risk of putting your authentic self out there and daring to be different. And, of course, if you genuinely enjoy blending into the background and living a low-key life, then there is nothing wrong with that whatsoever. Indeed, if you have chosen to live this way because it's what makes you genuinely happy and fulfilled, then you are living your best life and I salute you for it!

But (and that is a very big but!), if you are only conforming because you are terrified of being rejected, bullied or singled out as an individual, then **you need to know that taking comfort in conformity will never bring you true happiness in life**. If your life is driven by a desire to avoid rejection, then your life will become nothing but one long struggle against your authentic self!

The truth is this: **the more that you try and hide who you are, the unhappier you become.** If you chase conformity rather than cultivating individuality, you will never fulfil your true potential or find genuine happiness as a human being.

In the New Testament, Jesus teaches his followers this: **'No one lights a lamp and puts it in a place where it will be hidden, or under a bowl. Instead, they put it on its stand, so that those who come in may see the light' (Luke 12:33).** We need to recognise that we are each a powerful and precious light - you have the opportunity to become a beacon of positivity, love and authenticity in this world. So stop hiding away and desperately trying to blend in - choose instead to become fearlessly authentic!

It could not be clearer: **in order to live a happy life, you need to stop chasing conformity and start cultivating authenticity.** Indeed, **you can only live a genuinely happy, fulfilling and enriching life when you are unapologetically living as your authentic self.**

That is because it is only when we dare to express ourselves as unique individuals and unapologetically live life as our authentic selves that we are finally able to fulfil our potential. As John Stuart Mill says, **"it is only the cultivation of individuality which produces, or can produce, well-developed human beings".**

Being an authentic individual is nothing to apologise for – your uniqueness is in fact a cause for celebration! I cannot stress this enough: the only reason anyone is ever justified in criticising or rebuking you is if you are actively causing intentional harm to somebody else.

As long as you are not hurting anybody, you do not have to explain yourself to anyone. Whilst people do indeed have a right to pass judgment on every single aspect of your appearance, personality or identity, **you do not have to take their judgments to heart!** Do not give other people's narrow-minded and judgmental opinions about you one single second of your attention! It is one of my golden rules in life to never take criticism from someone I wouldn't take advice from. We all need to **stop holding back because we are scared of what other people will think of us.** Stop apologising for being 'too much' or for being 'different'. Instead, start realising that your uniqueness is something to celebrate, *not something you have to apologise for!*

If someone cannot accept you for who you authentically are, it is there problem and not yours. If someone cannot accept you living as your authentic self, then they do not deserve to be in your life.

Remember this - as long as you are not causing anybody else any harm, you have absolutely nothing to apologise for. Hold your head up high and know your unconditional worth. **This is your one life – and you deserve to live it to the absolute full!**

You - just as much as anybody else - deserve to experience the genuine happiness that comes from cultivating individuality and fulfilling your unique potential. So stop apologising and start thriving!

Dare to unapologetically live your truth.

Dare to become genuinely proud of who you authentically are.

4. KNOW YOUR VALUES & PRINCIPLES

"Never shirk the proper dispatch of your duty, no matter if you are freezing or hot, groggy or well-rested, vilified or praised, not even if dying or pressed by other demands. Even dying is one of the most important assignments of life and, in this as in all else, make the most of your resources to do well the duty at hand" (Marcus Aurelius)

To live a truly fulfilling life, you must live with absolute authenticity and integrity.

In life, we must - at all times - be true to ourselves and ensure we that we are *always* living in accordance with our core values and moral principles.

Never compromise your integrity for the sake of pleasing or impressing others!

Never hide your authentic self in a desperate attempt at to gain approval!

And never forget your morals or lose sight of what is truly important in your life, regardless of what other people may say and think.

There is nothing more important in life than being true to yourself. And I passionately believe that **being true to yourself begins with being true to your core values and principles.**

One of the reasons that I chose to study religion and philosophy at university was because of my obsession with 'human morality'. I am absolutely fascinated by the way in which different societies have created rules, regulations and moral codes to which their people are obliged to adhere. I am intrigued by how our deepest beliefs and principles shape how we live our whole entire lives.

In the past, people have turned to religion as their authoritative moral guide and compass for life. And so for centuries, religious teachings guided humanity and dictated to us what is 'right' and what is 'wrong'. The Church has maintained a total monopoly over western morality for hundreds of years - the things that we believe today about sex, marriage, and the value of human life have all been shaped by hundreds of years of Christian Church teachings.

Yet we are currently living through a time of unprecedented change. Belief in God is plummeting to its lowest levels in history, with people abandoning the religious beliefs and practices that had shaped human societies for hundreds of years. In the 21st century, religion no longer plays a powerful and authoritative role as the dictator of morality and the judge of human behaviour. We no longer look to the Church for moral guidance and knowledge - religion no longer has a monopoly on morality! So where do we look instead? Where do people today find their sense of morality? How do they determine that difference between right and wrong? In today's individualistic culture, people look within themselves!

This is an extraordinary 21st century phenomenon: morality

no longer comes from God or from a religious Holy Book, but must be determined by our own individual minds! Yes, in today's world we must find our sense of right and wrong from *within ourselves*. This gives us an extraordinary amount of freedom - we are no longer being told what to do by the Church, but are instead allowed to decide for ourselves how we will live our lives. Repression and suppression have been left behind - we live in the age of personal freedom and moral autonomy! But with all this freedom comes responsibility. That's because **every individual in the liberal western world must now take full responsibility for every single moral decision that they make.**

As the authors of our own moral codes, **we are completely accountable for everything that we do - the power is entirely in our own hands!** As Immanuel Kant once said, 'your principle of action [be made a law] for the whole world'. When we are act, we are sending a message to the whole entire world about what we think correct moral conduct looks like. In every decision that you make, you are sending a signal to the entire world about what it means to live a 'good life'. You are to be held accountable for every single thing that you do. and to be held as responsible for every single decision that you make. You cannot blame God and you cannot claim that you were just following the rules...**you are responsible for making your own rules!**

We must therefore be absolutely certain about what morals we - as an individual - stand for. As independent and autonomous moral agents, **we have a duty to know exactly what values we believe in and what principles we strive to live our lives by.**

The success of your personal brand is totally dependent on your ability to know - and live by - a strong set of core values and moral principles.

Your values and principles tell the world exactly who you are and exactly what you stand for as a person. They go to the very heart of what makes you an authentic and autonomous individual.

In order to be a success in life, it is essential that you know your core values and moral principles. You need to live and breathe these values and principles. You need to allow them to influence and infuse into every single thing that you do and every single decision that you make.

In my life, for example, everything I do is inspired by my guiding principle - to *'aspire to inspire'.* This is my personal motto and mission statement for life. In absolutely everything that I do, I consciously *'aspire to inspire'.*

Living my life by this key principle gives me the most incredible sense of purpose and integrity. It makes me feel like I am actually achieving something in my life and that every single day I am travelling one step further on my journey to becoming the very best version of myself.

Even if we do not identify as religious, **we should care about living a morally good life**, and that means striving to live our lives with a real sense of purpose and integrity.

It is your duty to conduct yourself as a responsible citizen who is guided by a strong set of core values and anchored in a strong set of moral principles.

Without these strong sets of core values and moral principles, we become weak and purposeless human beings.

Without these strong and unshakeable beliefs that give real

meaning and purpose to our lives, we would be unable to bear the heavy burdens that life places on our shoulders.

In the Book of Proverbs, we are taught that "When the storm has swept by, the wicked are gone, but the righteous stand firm for ever" (Proverbs 10:25).

We are also taught that "The prospect of the righteous is joy...but the hopes of the wicked come to nothing" (Proverbs 10:28).

It could not be clearer: **In order to live a meaningful, fulfiling and resilient life, you need to be guided by strong core values and you need to be anchored in a strong set of moral principles.**

 As well as 'aspiring to inspire', I also try to live my life in accordance with John Stuart Mill's 'Non-Harm Principle'. As you may remember, this is the idea that each person is absolutely free to do whatever makes them genuinely happy in life, as long as they are not causing harm to anybody else.

Every individual therefore has a right to the freedom of expression and also a right to protection from harm. I believe that intentionally causing harm to any human being is always unequivocally wrong.

Living my life by the 'non-harm' principle gives me the most extraordinary confidence to do more of the things that make me genuinely happy. It gives me the most incredible strength in the face of any rudeness or unkind judgement that I might encounter, and it reassures me that I am perfectly entitled to be living unashamedly as my authentic self.

There's one more moral principle that I think goes to the core of what I stand for as an individual, and that is the concept of 'equality'.

Equality is the idea that every single human life is of absolutely equal value. I passionately believe in the principle of 'equal opportunity' - every single individual should have an absolutely equal opportunity to succeed and thrive through life. It is grossly unfair that your background, ethnicity, sexuality, religion or household income could restrict your access to life-enhancing opportunities.

There should be a level-playing field for every single human being. Living with a commitment to the principle of equality means believing that every single person has an unshakeable right to the freedom of thought, speech, and self-expression.

This inspires me to speak out against human rights violations and acts of injustice, which allows me to feel like I am actively making a positive difference in our world.

In order to find fulfilment as human beings, it is so important that we speak up for what we believe in and stand up for the causes that we are passionate about.

As Gandhi once said, you must aspire to **'be the change you wish to see in the world'.**

Knowing your core values and principles means knowing exactly what you stand for as a human being. Our principles tell us everything we need to know about what kind of people we are and what we most care about in this world. **Nothing is more important than establishing your core values and principles and at all times being true to them.**

You should therefore have the courage to be true to your principles. Stand up for what you believe in and conduct yourself at all times with real moral integrity. **Stop worrying about what other people think and start focusing on living by your**

principles and values.

Do not bend over backwards for someone just because they are able to shout louder than you. Do not just agree with an opinion because you don't want to offend anyone or get caught up in confrontation. **Aspire at all times to conduct yourself as an autonomous individual with real moral integrity. Be anchored in your principles and be guided by your values.**

It is, of course, very important to remember that not everybody in the world will share the same moral principles and core values as you. This is absolutely nothing to worry about - we are all capable of co-existing alongside people we don't always agree with.

In the 21st century, an age characterised by a commitment to personal freedom and autonomy, no-one should ever feel under an obligation to conform. And that includes you! Make it your mission to stop blindly conforming to the crowd. **Establish for yourself what is truly important in your own life.**

Be true to yourself, think for yourself, and - most importantly - **be true to your values and principles**. You are a unique, autonomous human being who must take complete responsibility how you live your life. **This all begins with taking responsibility for your core values and moral principles.**

As Marcus Aurelius wrote 2,000 years ago, **'Dig deep within yourself, for there is a fountain of goodness ever ready to flow if you will keep digging'.** We cannot outsource responsibility for the decisions that we make to a religious leader or even to God Himself. Instead, we need to take full responsibility for our own morality!

Instead of just following the crowd and accepting what others tell you as the truth, **you must be confident enough to iden-**

tify and live by your own moral principles and values.

20th century philosopher Jean-Paul Sartre once wrote that **'man is condemned to be free; because once thrown into the world, he is responsible for everything he does'**. We are not born with a pre-existing purpose or an innate sense of morality. We are not pre-programmed with knowledge about right and wrong - we must figure it all out for ourselves. This gives us the most extraordinary amount of individual freedom.

Because we are born as this blank slate, we have an incredible opportunity to shape our entire lives in whatever way we choose. **But we must always remember that with this freedom comes responsibility.**

As autonomous individuals, we must take full responsibility for every decision that we take and every choice that we make. And this commitment to autonomy and responsibility all begins with taking responsibility for our core values and moral principles.

At all times, remember that you are accountable for the way in which you live your life. You have a responsibility to conduct yourself with moral integrity. That means you must **stop following the crowd and instead find your voice as an autonomous individual!**

Don't be silenced by a social media mob or the 21st century cancel culture - be loud and proud about what you believe to be true.

You can compromise on many things in life, but you must never compromise on your core values and principles!

Make it your mission to live a positive and fulfiling life that is guided by your core values and confidently anchored in your moral principles...

5. MAKE LOVE YOUR SUPREME GUIDING LIGHT

"Love is the ultimate and the highest goal to which man can aspire…the salvation of man is through love and in love" (Viktor Frankl)

Of all the core values that we can choose to live our lives by, I passionately believe that the most important, by far, is love. Indeed, I would argue that love is the supreme and universal value by which every single human being should strive to live their lives by.

Love is our universal guiding light. It is recognisable and powerful in all four corners of the world. **Love goes to the very core of what it means to be a human being.**

When we talk about 'love', we must make clear exactly what type of love it is that we are referring to. According to the Ancient Greeks, **there are seven different types of love experienced and expressed by human beings**.

They are:

- Agape – Selfless love, the kind of love spoken about by Christianity
- Philia – Affectionate love, such as between two

good friends. Based on genuine care and affection.

- Storge – Familial love, the love found within a family. Often begins in childhood, when a baby is dependent on their caregivers – love and care is essential for their survival.
- Pragma – Long-term and enduring love. A 'practical' kind of love that values the practical aspects of a relationship. May be seen as 'business-like' and transcends both the physical and causal. A mutually beneficial relationship like a strong business partnership.
- Philautia – Love of the self
- Eros – Love of the body, physical attraction towards another. The sexual kind of love.
- Ludus – Playful or 'game playing' love. Typically expressed through flirtation or seduction. Sees love as a 'challenge' or a 'game' to be played – it is uncommitted and 'just a bit of fun'.

As you can see, the term 'love' refers to an incredibly broad spectrum of human behaviours and experiences.

It is important for human beings to have experience of all seven different kids of love in order to enjoy a balanced life. Yet it is obvious that when we are talking about love **as a guiding light**, we are not referring to a life driven by the 'eros' (sexual) or 'ludus' (playful) expressions of love!

Whilst there is absolutely nothing wrong with these expressions of love, but we have to realise that they are motivated solely by selfish and physical desires. They are very animalistic in nature and would be classified as one of JS Mill's 'Lower Pleasures'. And so whilst they may bring us temporary pleasure or gratification, on their own they will never be able to bring us the genuine fulfilment and contentment that we all crave in our lives. **We have to be sure to know the distinction between selfish lust and unconditional love!**

I therefore believe that you should aspire to live a life that is guided and illuminated by the soverign light of agape love. **Agape Love is our greatest source of happiness, strength and purpose in our earthly lives. It gives our lives real meaning and fulfilment. It allows us to connect with people, care for those most in need, and come together as one humanity.**

Agape Love facilitates compassion and kindness whilst providing us with the strongest of foundations for the formation of meaningful relationships.

St Paul described agape love best in his letter to the Corinthians. He wrote: **"love is patient, love is kind. It does not envy, it does not boast, it is not proud. It does not dishonour others, it is not self-seeking, it is not easily angered, it keeps no record of wrongs. Love does not delight in evil but rejoices with the truth. It always protects, always trusts, always hopes, always perseveres. Love never fails"** (1 Corinthians 13:4-8).

There is no greater power in this world than agape love. There is nothing more powerful or important. It unites, heals and empowers people like no other force known to mankind.

Our hearts are so deeply lost without agape love. We cannot even *consider* seeking happiness or contentment in life if we are not living an existence enriched and illuminated by the guiding light of love. As Viktor Frankl writes, **love is 'the ultimate and highest goal to which man can aspire'.**

That's right, **love is the ultimate and highest goal in all of our**

lives. It also provides the foundation for the most important rule known to mankind...the Golden Rule! This universal rule, taught by Jesus Christ 2,000 years ago, commands us to **"Love your neighbour as yourself"**. There is no commandment or rule greater than this.

It is this religious expression of **'agape' love that is truly the most powerful and incredible force known to mankind.** This agape love motivates people to transcend their personal interests and physical desires in order to serve others through living a life of kindness and compassion.

This love is grounded in a genuine care for all of humanity and an unconditional love for all human beings. It is this extraordinarily selfless and unconditional love alone that can offer us true healing, happiness and fulfilment as human beings. You must therefore make it your mission in life to **fill every single day of your life with genuine and meaningful expressions of love. Make it you mission to make the most of every single opportunity you have to show kindness, compassion & appreciation.**

May we make love the ultimate goal towards which we all aspire in life.

May it guide us, inspire us, and illuminate everything that we do.

At all times, may love be our universally supreme guiding light.

In what seem to be even the darkest of times, always know that love will never let you down.

At all times, always remember these immortal words from St Paul: **Love never fails.**

6. PURSUE YOUR TRUE PASSIONS

"Follow your passion. It will lead to your purpose" (Oprah Winfrey)

Nothing fills human beings with greater joy than following their true passions and fulfilling their authentic purpose in life. Nothing can make the human heart more content or the human soul feel more complete than living and breathing your biggest passions.

For just one minute, I want you to stop thinking about what will make you popular, powerful, or will impress your parents. Stop thinking about what society – or other people in your life – expect you to do. Stop thinking about what you 'need' to do in order to win other people's acceptance and approval.

Instead, think about what truly excites YOU in life. What are you genuinely passionate about? What subjects could you talk about for hours? What hobbies and interests could keep you busy all night?

As human beings, we spend so much time trying to fit into boxes and impress other people. We follow the rules, conform to the stereotypes, and keep in line with the customs of our culture.

This is all very well, as long as following the crowd genuinely brings you happiness and contentment. Indeed, for many people, it is very helpful to have these societal guidelines and cultural expectations about how you should live your life. I do not doubt that many people - perhaps the vast majority of the population- are quite happy following the crowd and conforming.

But others do not feel quite so satisfied with this life of custom and conformity. Some of us find that we have passions and interests which don't necessarily fall into line with the stereo-types promoted by society.

The problem with taking comfort in conformity is that it will only ever make you happy in the short term. You might be able to temporarily fake an interest in football or lie about loving a certain lifestyle – but only for so long. Eventually, you will start to realise just how deeply unfulfilled and disen-franchised you feel.

Because whilst conformity may provide protection and com-fort, we only become the best version of ourselves when we stop caring what about what other people think and start doing more of the things that truly make us happy instead.

We only find ourselves and become genuinely happy in life when we forget following the status quo and **invest time and effort into pursuing our real passions.**

Pursuing your passions awakens you to a higher calling and guides you towards a guaranteed source of fulfilment in your life. Whether that is a sport, a subject, a hobby, or something else entirely, **you owe it to yourself to pursue your passions and live your most authentic and fulfilling life!**

 In my case, for example, I am ridiculously passionate about philosophy and psychology. I make no secret of my obsession with these subjects and make no effort to conceal the fact that I am at my happiest when engaged in deep conversation or debate with a good cup of tea (or a large glass of prosecco) in hand! Nothing makes me happier than reading about current affairs and browsing the opinion pieces in the newspapers, before then talking to people about their own opinions on these ideas and discussion points. **It is not enough to just know what your passion is – you've got to live and breathe it every single day of your life!**

And so in my life, I try to channel my passions online – I write a blog on philosophy and psychology, film YouTube videos teaching A Level Philosophy, and tweet philosophical quotes no less than ten thousand times a day. Nothing excites me more than doing all these YouTube videos – I love buying the lighting equipment, writing the scripts, filming the content, and hearing from people who have enjoyed them.

It is something that I really do absolutely love and – crucially – it is something that I feel contributes to the common good of humanity. It makes me feel like I'm making a difference and that I'm turning my passion into something productive – which gives me a real sense of purpose in my life.

As my favourite philosopher of all time John Stuart Mill wrote back in 1859, **"In proportion to the development of his individuality, each person becomes more valuable to himself, and is, therefore, capable of becoming more valuable to others"**.

When we pursue our true passions and achieve our full potential, **we are able to make our best possible contributions to the common good of society.** I take great pride in my bookshelf lined with books by my favourite philosophers (JS Mill, of course, alongside Kant, Aristotle and Sartre!) and I look for every opportunity to drop one of their quotes into my conversations! I like to think that by sharing my love for philosophy with the world, I am able to educate and empower people to become the best version of themselves.

Nothing excites me more than learning new ideas in philosophy and being able to teach other people about them. I love the idea that through conversation I can both educate and empower both myself and the people around me! I've found a real passion for conversation, debate, learning, reading, writing, and teaching. And as a result, I wake up every morning genuinely excited for the day ahead!

This is what I believe: **In order to live a genuinely happy and deeply fulfilling life, we need to find purpose by pursuing our passions. In order to become the best version of yourself, you need to find ways of turning your passions into something productive that can make a positive difference in the world!**

For example, Is there a project you could work on? Is there a career path you could follow that would allow you to turn your passions into a source of income?

When you pursue your passions, you breathe new energy into your entire existence. You experience a buzz like no other and become truly energised by a real sense of purpose. As George Lorimer once said, **'You've got to get up every morning with determination if you're going to go to bed with satisfaction'.** Hal Elrod puts it like this: "When you wake up each day with passion and purpose, you join the small percentage of high achievers who are living their dreams. Most importantly, you will be happy". It could not be clearer - you should make it your mission to wake up every single day feeling excited to pursue your passions and ready to live your very best life!

Living a meaningful and fulfiling life all starts with getting passionate about pursuing your passions! Geek out on the subjects that you love. Invest time and energy into doing the things that genuinely interest you. Most importantly, don't feel that you need to always fit in or that you can only ever do things that other people will approve of.

Remember that this is your one life, and you deserve to spend all of it doing more of the things that bring you genuine happiness and fulfillment!

7. PERSEVERANCE IS KEY

"If the answer is no, you're talking to the wrong person" (Kris Jenner)

Far too many people give up far too easily. When they fall at the first hurdle, they simply admit defeat and go home rather than giving it another go. So much potential is wasted and so many opportunities are missed because people quit trying before they've even properly got started.

If you want to succeed in this world, there are three things you cannot afford to be afraid of: other people's opinions, hard work, and failure.

And you cannot expect success to be an instant and overnight phenomenon – **the road to success is a journey of overcoming obstacles, struggling through setbacks, and conquering difficult challenges.**

As the multi-billionaire founder of Amazon Jeff Bezos is reported to have once said, '**every overnight success story was 10 years in the making**'.

It takes blood, sweat, and tears to get to the top – and it takes even more of all three of these to stay there!

Whilst it's very easy to become extremely disheartened by having to go through adversity, those who truly want enjoy success in life know the importance of taking setbacks on the chin. **When one route to success doesn't work out, you do whatever it takes to find another one.**

Just because Plan A didn't work out, that doesn't mean you should just give up on all of your dreams and ambitions! As John D Rockefeller once remarked, **'I do not think there is any other quality so essential to success of any kind as the quality of perseverance. It overcomes almost everything, even nature'.**

Those who make it to the top of their fields and turn their dreams into their reality are not necessarily the most talented people in the room. In music, for example, the artists you see at the top of the charts are not necessarily the best singers in the world. The artists who make it to the top are those who are prepared to be more ambitious, hard-working and resilient than anybody else.

As Jennifer Lopez recently said, 'you've got to work harder than anybody else'. You could be the most amazing singer in the universe, but if you don't know have the drive and ambition to turn that talent into a successful career, then you're not going to be headlining Glastonbury anytime soon! **Without effort and perseverance, talent remains nothing more than unfulfilled potential – and what is the point of having any of that?**

Remember what Aristotle teaches us - **in order to achieve happiness in life, we need to get serious about fulfilling our potential as human beings!**

And the secret to fulfilling your potential is discovering your passions and persevering until you make a success of them!

Angela Duckworth, a psychologist who believes 'passion and perseverance are the secrets to success', says this: **"As much as** talent counts, effort counts twice".

In other words, **You might have the talent, but what matters is how you put it to good use.** To fulfil your potential and put your talents into practice, you've got to commit to living a life of hard work, perseverance and dedication!

You cannot expect success to be handed to you on a plate - achievement in this world requires nothing less than blood, sweat, tears and perseverance!

Let's explore this a little further. **Experts tell us that it takes 10,000 hours of practice to become an expert at something.** You can't just sit down at the piano for the first time and expect to become a concert-level pianist within the first 30 minutes! **When it comes to turning your dreams into your reality, effort is absolutely everything!**

An essential element of effort is **your ability to overcome adversity**. You need to be willing to confront all of the challenges that you face in your life head-on, and remember my mantra: **whatever happens in life, you can handle it!**

Let's be very clear – no one's journey to success is ever going to be a gentle walk in the park! You are never going to achieve anything worthwhile overnight - success is not a 'quick fix' situation!

When it comes to your journey towards achievement and success in life, I can guarantee there will be countless bumps in the road and a relentless stream of setbacks that may threaten to throw you off course. The important thing is that you **keep the bigger picture behind your journey in mind and that you therefore recognise the importance of perseverance.**

You need to passionately believe in what you are doing and realise that what you are doing has real purpose behind it. You cannot give up at the first hurdle and you cannot quit when it all gets too much. Instead, you need to believe that what you are doing is too important to ever quit! When you believe so strongly in your cause, you become fearless about putting yourself out there and bouncing back from every single setback that you face!

Every time you get knocked down, you have no option but to pick yourself up and get straight back in the game. So have a cup of tea, have a good cry - and then get straight back into battle!

Remember, every setback is sent by the universe to teach us an essential life lesson. *You grow through what you go through, and you cannot enjoy success in life if you have not overcome setbacks along the way!*

The secret to living with this undefeatable spirit of perseverance – and remember, it is this spirit that will allow you to overcome every single obstacle and setback that you face in your life – **is to live your life with a real sense of purpose.**

You need to believe very strongly in what it is you are trying to achieve. **That means being guided at all times by the key question - 'What's worth doing even if I fail?'** For example, you might be training to become a teacher because you want to are passionate about transforming young lives. You might be starting a campaign and petition because you believe that you have a duty to bring about change in a certain area of social policy. Or you might be trying to build your start-up business because you passionately want to create a brighter future for your family.

One thing is clear: the secret to living with an undefeatable spirit of perseverance is living with a strong sense of purpose.

It is this sense of purpose – which is all about the 'why' behind what we are doing – that keeps us going when the going gets tough.

It is this sense purpose that fuels the 'grit' that we all need in order to remain resilient no matter what challenges and obstacles we face.

I believe very strongly that this 'grit' is the *essential* ingredient that we all need in order to get where we want to be in life.

Angela Duckworth writes this:

"Grit is sticking with your future, day in, day out, not just for the week, not just for the month, but for years, and working hard to make that future a reality. Grit is living life like it's a marathon, not a sprint".

You cannot give something a go for a few days and then just give up when things don't work out as planned. You cannot just dip your toe in the pool for five seconds and then run a mile when you realise that the water is too cold. **To achieve your dreams and fulfil your potential in life, you need to see the bigger picture behind what you're doing and become absolutely committed to living life with real purpose and perseverance.**

As you know, I very strongly believe that the process is just as important as the final product! Perserverance is all about being able to think 'long term' and keep your eyes fixed on the bigger purpose behind what you're doing. You need to be passionate about 'walking your why' and living with a real sense of purpose **every single day of your life.**

Remember, what appeared to be an overnight success was actually 10 years in the making! There is no quick-fix solution to living a happy and fulfiling life! You need to know your life's purpose and have perserverance on your journey through every single day!

The truth is this: **we need to enjoy the journey just as much as we enjoy the final product.** If we want to turn our dreams into our reality, then we need to be prepared to persevere through all kinds of obstacles and challenges.

If you genuinely believe in your dreams and feel a real sense of purpose about what you are doing, then I have every confidence that you will be able to turn all of your dreams into your reality. **With passion and perseverance, I strongly believe that anything is possible. So no matter what you are going through, keep going! Keep picking yourself up, keep bouncing back, and keep focused on your final destination!**

Let me say it once more: whatever you're going through, KEEP GOING! It's time to get serious about living a life of purpose, passion and perseverance!

8. ADVERSITY FORGES CHARACTER

"I judge you unfortunate if you have never lived through misfortune. You have passed through life without an opponent – no one can ever know what you are capable of, not even you" (Seneca)

If there is anything that I know for sure, it is that you should never be afraid of going through tough times.

There is no challenge too difficult for us to get through, and there is no struggle too great that you cannot bear the burden. No matter what it is that you're dealing with in life, remember that you can handle it.

Tough times are character building. We need to go through failures, setbacks, and suffering in order to grow as human beings. We cannot hide from painful experiences – **no one promised you that life would be easy or free from pain! Instead, we have no choice but to bear life's burdens with as much courage, dignity, and resilience as we can.**

It is essential that you stoically accept the fact that suffering is an inevitable part of life. As His Holiness the Dalai Lama writes, **"It is important to accept suffering as a natural fact of human existence"**. In the western world, **we have attempted to suppress and avoid suffering rather than re-**

sponding to it with courage and resilience.

As you know, I believe that in every single area of our lives, *attitude is everything!* Our default attitude towards suffering consists of an intense aversion and intolerance of all pain. This is extremely damaging, because it leads to us becoming utterly incapable of dealing with the suffering we will all inevitably face in our lives.

However, if we can transform our attitude towards suffering and adopt an attitude that allows us greater tolerance of it, then this can do much to help challenge the feelings of dissatisfaction and discontentment that we experience in our lives. We need to make a very clear distinction between the pain of pain (which is real) and the pain we create by our thoughts about the pain (which we create in our own minds).

Fear, anger, and helplessness are all emotional responses that can unnecessarily intensify the feeling of pain. **It is our responsibility to counteract these emotions with a greater tolerance of suffering** – it's time to stop struggling against suffering and **start finding meaning in adversity instead!**

Dr. Paul Brand, author of the book 'Pain: The Gift Nobody Wants', writes that **"the attitude we cultivate in advance may well determine how suffering will affect us when it does strike".** We need to stop seeing suffering as something to be avoided at all costs and start seeing it as **an opportunity for personal growth and development.**

Albert Einstein once remarked that **"in the middle of difficulty lies opportunity".** Here's what I passionately believe: **Stop struggling against suffering and start seeing adversity as a gift!**

Our biggest obstacles are our best teachers – we have to allow every obstacle to teach us just what resilient individ-

uals we really are!

When we see someone suffering, we might remark 'I couldn't cope with that' or 'I don't know how you do it'. When we hear about some incredible feat someone has achieved, we comment that 'Never in a million years would I be able to do that'.

What I want to ask is this – why not? Are we not all human beings? Do we not all have the same capability to make choices, take risks, and follow our dreams? It all comes down to whether you are prepared to put yourself out there and take setbacks in your stride.

Finding confidence in life is all about realising that the only way to become the best version of yourself is by making mistakes and learning from them.

 The road to success begins with an acknowledgment of the fact that you will face adversity in your life, but with a realisation that you will be more than capable of handling it. You will not just survive the criticism and challenges that you face, but you will find ways of thriving because of them!

<u>Every obstacle and challenge that you face in life will become a catalyst for self-growth!</u> Remember what I always say - **you grow through what you go through!** Adversity is essential for the formation of character.

We can only properly appreciate our successes in life when we have also been through suffering and experienced failure. *You only appreciate the safety of the harbour once you have battled through the dangerously choppy waters out at sea!*

As an avid book reader I find it helpful to think of life as like a good book. Allow me to elaborate! When you pick up any good novel, do you expect every single page to be filled with happiness and joy? Do you expect the whole book to be the 'happy ever after'? I think that would make for a very boring 400 or so pages, don't you?!

With a good novel, we expect adversity. What's more, we see that the heroes of the story NEED to go through that adversity in order to develop into the characters that we love. Without those setbacks, struggles, and challenges, our fictional heroes would not be able to realise their potential and showcase their bravery to the world!

Without being tested and challenged, the fictional characters we love and admire would never have the chance to actually become these strong, moral and heroic characters we love!

The universal truth is this: **adversity forges character!** Suffering is essential for our growth! Every setback that we face is yet another opportunity to bounce back stronger. It is the Universe's way of teaching us to learn from our mistakes and become an even better version of ourselves.

Setbacks are a gift from the universe reminding us that we have more strength and resilience than we ever thought! Just like the leading characters in your favourite novels or films, you need to face adversity in order to develop your character! You cannot become the best version of yourself without experiencing struggles, setbacks, and failures. You cannot fulfil your potential if you have not learned from mistakes and faced challenges along the way.

History teaches us that **out of suffering has emerged the strongest of souls**. There is not a single person on this entire planet that has not been through suffering. You cannot enjoy success if you have not also been subjected to suffering. **We** must all endure tough times and be subjected to painful ex-perience – this is, whether we like it or not, just a brutal fact of human life.

As a result, we shouldn't fight against suffering or fear having to go through adversity. Instead, we should **try to actively embrace every single challenge that we face in life and see it as a welcome opportunity to become an even better version of yourself!** *What doesn't kill you, so they say, makes you stronger.*

When it comes to facing suffering, we are confronted with two very clear choices: We can choose either to struggle against reality and refuse to accept the fact that suffering is a normal part of life. Alternatively, we can choose to **accept the fact that suffering simply exists as a natural and normal part of every single person's life.**

When we learn to accept suffering as a natural and inevitable part of human life, **we transform every obstacle that we face in life into an opportunity.** We stop fighting against reality and start embracing every challenge as a chance to become more a courageous, resilient, and empowered human being. **As a result, we start realise that out of setbacks grow strong characters and out of suffering grows miracles.** *Suffering does not break souls but builds strong and resilient characters.*

As the Old Testament Book of Joshua commands us: **"Be strong and courageous; do not be frightened or dismayed!" (Joshua 1:9).**

The Buddhist monk Thich Nhat Hahn writes that **"without suffering, there is no happiness. So we shouldn't discriminate against the mud. We have to learn how to embrace and cradle our suffering and the suffering of the world, with a lot of tenderness".** We must be prepared to accept the existence of adversity - and resolve to handle every challenge we face with courage, resilience, and perseverance.

I don't like to be rude, but actually nobody promised you that life would be easy! **Nobody promised that everything would be plain-sailing from the second of your birth!** The only promise that exists is the promise you can make to yourself that you will take on every challenge you face with confidence, courage, and without complaint. **Stop fighting against life and complaining that isn't fair – embrace every challenge as a chance to grow and turn every obstacle into an opportunity!**

<u>**Adversity forges character and suffering strengthens souls. We grow in kindness when our kindness is tested.**</u>

There really is no better education than the endurance of hard times. **We need to totally transform our perspective on suffering, and this begins by ceasing to struggle against it.**

The great Roman Emperor and Stoic philosopher Marcus Aurelius wrote in his diaries that **"that which is an impediment to action is turned to advance action. The obstacle on the path becomes the way"**. The mind can adapt and convert any obstacle in its way into 'its means of achieving' your goal. In the least morbid way possible, unless you are dead then you can keep on going. *And If you are dead, then you've got nothing to worry about anyway!* So, as long as you are alive, you can always keep striving to become the best version of yourself and to live your very best life! That means taking on more risks, making even bigger mistakes, and always remembering to keep bouncing straight back!

As long as you are living your life with a real sense of purpose, you will be able to handle every single challenge that you face. In his excellent book 'The Miracle Morning', Hal Elrod writes this: **'When you are committed to a life purpose that is bigger than your problems, your problems become relatively insignificant and you will overcome them with ease'.** We should stop struggling against suffering and instead focus on growing through it.

Whatever happens in life, you can handle it. Remember that every setback brings you closer to success. Start seeing every obstacle you face as another opportunity to become an even better version of yourself!

Always remember that you grow through what you go through!

Adversity forges character, and tough times turn you into the very best version of yourself!

9. ASPIRE NOT TO HAVE MORE BUT TO BE MORE

"Don't judge each day by the harvest you reap but the seeds that you plant" (Popular Aphorism)

In our materialistic world, we are always wanting more and more. We have been brought up to believe that having more - more possessions, more approval, more social media followers - is the secret to living a happy life.

As a society, we have become obsessed with accumulation and we have become slaves to consumerism. We seem to believe that you can somehow 'buy' your way to happiness! This belief is, of course, completely wrong.

We all know full well that it is impossible to buy your way to happiness – having more possessions does not automatically lead to more happiness in your life. *You cannot just swipe your card and purchase fulfilment!*

Instead of mindlessly attempting to buy our way to happiness, we need to wake up to the realisation that happiness is produced through the cultivation of a meaningful and enriching life. In other words, happiness is achieved by 'aspiring not to have more but to be more'.

◆ ◆ ◆

So, what does it mean to 'aspire not to have more but to be more'? It means realising that **the secret to living a genuinely fulfilling life is to focus on cultivating good character rather than always wanting to acquire more possessions**. It is about fulfiling your potential and becoming the best version of yourself, rather than aimlessly striving to have the most expensive designer wardrobe or the biggest social media following.

Happiness is not just handed to you on a plate. Happiness cannot just be bought with your credit card. This is my passionate belief: **don't just sit there and pray for an easy life – get out there and work hard to create a meaningful one!**

The idea of aspiring to 'be more' is grounded in a realisation that <u>the only person you should ever compete with is who you were yesterday</u>. **To start living your best life, you need to stop being driven by envy and instead strive to become someone who is capable of inspiring others.**

It was St Oscar Romero, the Archbishop of El Salvador, who first taught that we should 'aspire not to have more but to be more' in our lives. Let me tell you a little bit about this remarkable man. Oscar Romero was famously assassinated for speaking out against human rights abuses, having dedicated his entire life to campaigning against social injustice and violence. He was a vocal critic of the government's violent treatment of its own people during El Salvador's civil conflict. Just one year before his assassination whilst saying Mass, Romero had been nominated for the Nobel Peace Prize in response to his unreserved advocacy of human rights.

He had most notably made outspoken defences of the poor – who were the powerless victims of the widespread violence in El Salvador – and had dedicated his life to helping those most in need. His life story showcases a man who put his faith and beliefs into practice, and was even prepared to lose his own life as a result of speaking out against oppression.

I strongly believe that we should all **aspire to become this kind of inspiring character.** In other words, we should all aspire to become empowered individuals who actively make a positive difference in this world.

Our lives should be dedicated not to the pursuit of selfish desires but instead to the defence and empowerment of the most vulnerable and oppressed. **We should strive to help others in any way that we can, and strive to 'be the change [that] we wish to see in the world'.**

In the Book of Proverbs, we are taught that **"One person gives freely, yet gains even more; another withholds unduly, but becomes poverty"** (Proverbs 12:24). We are also taught: **"A generous person will prosper; whoever refreshes others will be refreshed"** (Proverbs 12:25).

It could not be clearer - it is through giving to others that we will receive ourselves! We should stop being so selfish and start being more selfless! By aspiring not to have more but to be more, you are able to start living your very best life and fulfil your potential as a socially-conscious and moral human being!

In order to start 'becoming more' as a person, you need ask yourself these key questions: Who do I want to be as a person? How can I aspire others through my actions? How can I make a difference in people's lives? What skills can I use in the service of humankind? How can I empower others to become the best version of themselves?

Each of us has a unique set of skills, talents and attributes. St

Paul writes in his letter to the Corinthians that **'each has his own gift from God'.** Life is all about discovering what your unique talents are (because I have no doubt that you have more than one!!) and working out how you can use them to make the world a better place!

The purpose of your life is to start fulfilling your potential by making a positive difference on this planet!

We should all aspire to use our gifts and talents in ways that will serve and benefit the world. Ask yourself this: **what skills might I be able to bring to the table and how might I be able to use my talents to help those most in need?**

My personal mission statement in life is to **'aspire to inspire'.** Every single day, I strive to inspire people to take control of their life and become the best version of themselves.

The reason I do this is because I know exactly what it is like to be at your lowest and most helpless point. Several years ago, I was hospitalised with the eating disorder anorexia and told by my doctors that I was going to die. As well as this, I have for many years battled with accepting my sexual orientation and have faced daily barrages of homophobic comments and remarks.

Despite these setbacks, I am here today living what I genuinely believe to be my very best life. I am studying the course of my dreams in the city of my dreams, and I am busy doing all of the things that I have always dreamed of doing! I've ticked off everything on my bucket list - and more!

And now, I want to show anyone that might be in that 'rock bottom' place that **there is a light at the end of the tunnel** . I want to show people that with hard-work and perseverance, you *can* turn your life around! You can turn all of your dreams into your new reality! *As I always say, if I can do it, then so can* *you!*

I am so proud to be living my best and most authentic life, and **it is my biggest aspiration in life to inspire as many people as possible to do the same!** If I can inspire just one young person struggling to find their place in this world to have a little bit more self-confidence and to start believing in their potential, then my work here is done!

Here's what I believe: **You were born to make an impact.** Yes, YOU! You were put on this planet to make a real difference. **Every single day provides you with yet another opportunity to make that genuine difference in the lives of others.**

You can use your skills, talents and your voice to help those most in need. **You have the potential to become a beacon of light for people who are going through tough times! You have the potential to become a ray of sunshine in somebody's difficult and testing day!**

There is nothing more rewarding or fulfilling than knowing that you have made a difference in someone else's life. It is a feeling of pride and achievement that no amount of money can buy - *so stop aspiring to have more and start aspiring to become more*! As John D. Rockefeller Jr once said, you should "think of giving not as a duty, but as a privilege". Be deeply thankful for every single opportunity that you get to make a difference in somebody else's day!

When we commit to 'becoming more' as individuals, we quite literally transform our lives. Each day is no longer a struggle against suffering but suddenly becomes another step on your journey towards genuine fulfillment. **Obstacles suddenly become opportunities** and **challenges are transformed into**

chances to grow. We begin to realise that life is so much more fulfiling when we stop just 'surviving' through each week and start **THRIVING** through every single moment that we spend here on this planet!

I can honestly say that **there is nothing more rewarding or life-affirming than knowing that you have made a real difference in somebody else's day.** Nothing feels better than knowing that you have inspired someone to find self-confidence or that you have helped someone to overcome some kind of adversity in their life.

And so I urge you to **aspire to become somebody that inspires!** Not only will you change other people's lives, but you will also start instantly thriving in your own as well! Never tire of striving to become the best version of yourself in every single situation that you are faced with. Afterall, you cannot inspire other people to live their best lives if you are not living yours!

Remember, **Life is all about fulfilling your potential and flourishing as a human being!**

You are here on this planet to live a genuinely fulfilling life. As the Holocaust survivor Viktor Frankl wrote, **"What man actually needs is not a tensionless state but rather the striving and struggling for some goal worthy of him".** In other words, don't pray that your life is easy - work hard to ensure that your life is meaningful!

Let me say that again: **Life isn't meant to be easy - it is meant to be meaningful.** We should embrace every challenge that we face in our lives as a positive opportunity to 'become more' as an individual. As Frankl writes, the suffering we experience in life **"presents us with a challenge – to find our goals and purpose in our lives that make even the worst situation worth living through".**

We cannot find fulfillment in this life if we are focused solely on the pursuit of personal pleasure and worldly wealth. **The only way to live a truly enriching life is to live with a real sense of purpose.**

And this sense of purpose is is found in aspiring not to have more but to become more as an individual. And the more we *become* as meaning-seeking individuals, the happier we become as well!

Aspiring not to have more but to be more means consciously making an effort to live each day of our lives to the full, rather than just trying to get through them. 'Becoming more' means living with a real sense of purpose, presence and power as autonomous and authentic human beings.

So I urge you: Aspire to become more.

Aspire to become a beacon of light in times of darkness.

Aspire to stand up for what you believe in.

Aspire to make a meaningful difference in the lives of others.

Aspire to fulfill your potential and to become the very best version of yourself.

10. EMBRACE YOUR EMOTIONS

"When awareness is brought to an emotion, power is brought to your life" (Tara Meyer Robson)

Back in the 1970s, the psychologist Paul Eckman identified six basic emotions that he believed were universally experienced by all human beings. They are:

- Happiness
- Sadness
- Fear
- Disgust
- Anger
- Surprise.

 These 'basic emotions' are believed to form the building blocks for the whole rainbow of feelings that we all experience throughout our lifetimes. Psychologist Robert Plutchik theorised that humans experience a so-called 'wheel of emotions', which works just like the colour wheel taught about in art lessons!

According to this 'colour wheel' theory, **the six basic emotions can all be combined to form different feelings, in the same way that the different primary colours can be mixed to create more complex shades**. The emotions that we experience are never just black and white, and throughout our lives we will experience different emotions to different degrees and different intensities. Your emotions and feelings are very complex things!

Experiencing a whole spectrum of emotions is just part of being human. Despite this, **so many of us struggle to acknowledge, accept and intelligently manage our feelings.**

Some people, for example, try to entirely shut off from emotions and ban themselves from ever acknowledging or talking about how they are feeling.

Others take things to the opposite extreme and become utterly overwhelmed by every single emotion that they experience. They become like little sailboats on a stormy sea, are are regularly swept up and 'blown around' by every single feeling that they experience. As a result, they end up being unable to make rational decisions or respond to complex situations intelligently. Their decision-making processes become completely overwhelmed by strong emotional impulses over which they have absolutely no control.

Both of these examples demonstrate an emotional extreme. They demonstrate people becoming either completely *lacking* in any emotional expression whatsoever, or becoming totally *overwhelmed* by every single emotions, feelings and desire that they experience. Both of these approaches demonstrate a real lack of emotional intelligence. They are both recipes for disaster and will both serve as impenetrable barriers to personal happiness and flourishing.

Here's what I believe: **In order to live a happy and meaningful life, we need to get serious about cultivating emotional intelligence!**

Emotional intelligence is all about taking a rational, balanced and intelligent approach to your emotions. It is essential that we find a healthy and intelligent balance between the two extremes of emotional deficiency and emotional over-involvement. In other words, we need to get intelligent about our emotions and **aspire to live an emotionally intelligent life!**

So, what exactly does it mean to live an 'emotionally intelligent' life? Allow me to explain! **Emotional intelligence is all about intelligently acknowledging, accepting and managing your emotions.** Being 'emotionally intelligent' means **learning to acknowledge your feelings without being totally overwhelmed by them.** It means being able to listen to both your head and to your heart, before consciously choosing how you will respond to a situation.

In order to find happiness and stability in our lives, **we need to get comfortable with experiencing the full spectrum of emotions.** We need to get comfortable with feeling vulnerable and allowing ourselves acknowledge and validate every single feeling that arises within us.

In our society today, there seems to be a complete obsession with only ever experiencing 'positive' emotions , and a total fear of feeling anything 'negative'. *We seem to believe that we would not be able to cope if we let even the tiniest bit of sadness into our lives.* So many people seem to believe that they would be totally incapable of acknowledging feelings of fear or anger without being totally overwhelmed by these emotions. **Well I've got some news for you - having this amount of fear about your feelings is absolutely irrational!**

This is what you need to know: **whatever emotion you are experiencing, you can handle it.**

We need to make peace with the full spectrum of emotions that we experience as human beings and realise that it is perfectly natural to feel not only happiness but also sadness, fear, disgust, anger and surprise throughout our lives! **Our emo-**

tions should not be labelled as either 'positive' or 'negative' - they are all just simply part of who we are!

If we want to start living a genuinely happy and fulfiling life, we cannot continue struggling against our emotions. Instead, **we need to learn to acknowledge and experience every single one of our feelings, without being completely overwhelmed by them.** This means, for example, being able to acknowledge when you feel angry without being immediately compelled into impulsive action. And it means being able to acknowledge when you are feeling that paralysing sensation of fear... and then making yourself do the thing that was making you feel so scared anyway!

Emotional intelligence is the process of making peace with your emotions and realising that you do not have to be scared of them! It means realising that do not have to go through life as a slave to your feelings! **It means knowing with confidence that whatever emotion you are feeling right now, you can handle it.**

You do not need to fear your feelings! You do not need to become totally overwhelmed by your emotions, although you should also know that there is nothing to be embarrassed about if you sometimes are. **Your emotions – ALL of them - are simply reminders that you are a human being!** You must therefore give yourself *full permission* to acknowledge and accept every single one of them.

The golden rule of emotional intelligence is this: **stop fearing your feelings...and make friends with them instead!** Just because you have acknowledged an emotion, this doesn't mean that you are going to become completely overwhelmed by it!

There is no emotion that you cannot cope with, as long as you give yourself the space to acknowledge and experience it in a healthy way!

The more we try to suppress our true feelings, the more suffering we create for ourselves. **We need to provide our emotions with an outlet for expression and we need to get serious about giving ourselves the opportunity to healthily express how we feel.**

It's important for us to be aware that emotions don't just turn up for no reason; **they always have a valid origin within us.** In order to work out that origin, we need to get confident about acknowledging and making sense of them before taking positive steps towards intelligently managing them.

If we don't, they will start to eat away at us and limit our capacity to experience genuine happiness and fulfilment in life! **Always remember that there is nothing to be gained from bottling up your emotions.** Denying your feelings will always result in them causing even more destruction in your life. **The more we try to bury our feelings, the more dangerous they become.**

It is therefore esential that all of your emotions are wholeheartedly acknowledged and then healthily expressed, because they will otherwise just cause absolute chaos in your life! **Every feeling you experience must be accepted, acknowledged, and intelligently managed!**

Let me say it again: even your strongest emotions are nothing to fear. You can manage them all! **The emotion may be strong, but you are stronger!**

The more you struggle against your emotions, the more you will suffer – so just let yourself feel exactly what you are feeling. You are not going to be uncontrollably overwhelmed by your emotions just because you have acknowledged that they are there.

You must acknowledge and accept every single emotion that you are experiencing.

When you become aware of a certain emotion that you are feeling, you can choose to harness and express it in a healthy and intelligent way. For example, feeling anger about social injustice that you have witnessed may lead to you taking positive action to promote this important cause and speak out on a public platform. Meanwhile, experiencing sadness has been found by some studies to improve memory, judgment, motivation, and sometimes even to improve your competence in social interactions.

This gives me the confidence to believe that **Your emotions themselves are relatively neutral – it is how you choose to label, harness and respond to them that matters more than anything else.**

Whenever I recognise myself feeling a powerful emotion – especially one that has the potential to be overwhelming – I repeat this simple mantra: **'let it come, let it be, let it go'.**

Instead of struggling against the emotion, I acknowledge it. Instead of denying the feeling, I accept it. **This approach hands me the power to decide what happens next – I am now in control of how I express this emotion, rather than being controlled by the emotion itself.**

To live a truly fulfilling life, we must cultivate emotional intelligence. We need to acknowledge and accept our feelings. We need to talk about them and express them in healthy ways. That might be through art, sport, journaling or even through spiritual disciplines such as meditation and yoga!

Whatever you do, don't struggle against your emotions.

Struggle and suppression lead to just one thing – suffering. You need to save your energy for managing your feelings with real emotional intelligence!

Remember this: your emotions may be strong, but you are stronger. You can handle them and you are more than capable of healthily managing them! It's time to stop fearing your feelings and start intelligently making friends with ALL of your emotions instead....

11. WHAT OTHER PEOPLE THINK OF YOU IS NONE OF YOUR BUSINESS

"Confidence isn't thinking everyone will like you, it's knowing that you'll be just fine even if they don't" (Popular Aphorism)

What other people think of you is none of your business! It is shocking how many people spend their whole entire lives being held hostage to a paralysing fear of what other people – including complete strangers – think of them. They give themselves a life sentence to the prison of public opinion and become dependent on validation from others in order to feel good about themselves. **This is a toxic way to live and it is the perfect example of someone fighting a losing battle**.

The truth of life is this: **not everyone is going to like you....but you don't have to care!** No matter how hard you try, will never ever succeed at making other people like, love, understand, validate, accept or be nice to you. It's just not possible! Remember, the only thing you ever have control over in life is YOURSELF!

You have to accept that sometimes, you just will not be people's cup of tea! *Some people like a PG Tips, other people are more into their Tetley!* It's nothing personal - it's just a matter of personal preference! *And so you just have to get over it!*

We have to wake up to the fact that **we will never please or win approval of absolutely everyone.** *Never in a million years is it going to happen.* But guess what? You don't need to worry about it! Because whilst **people may indeed have the right to form an opinion about you, you have a right not to care!**

People form opinions about everything and everyone all the time. They make split-second judgments and appearance-based assessments all day, every day. It's just a fact of life that not all of these judgments are going to be favourable! In the same way that we prefer certain foods and certain places, we also just so happen to prefer certain people! Again, this is absolutely nothing personal! You are not being personally attacked or being universally disliked - you are just not every single person's cup of tea! *The chicken nuggets don't take it personally when you decide to have fish fingers for dinner, and in exactly the same way you must stop taking it so personally when you are not everybody's flavour of the month!* It is impossible to be universally liked and - more to the point - it is totally irrational to want to be universally liked in the first place!

The fact that some people do not like you does not matter in the slightest. In fact, I think it actually means that you're doing something *right.* Indeed, I am a strong believer that if nobody is taking a disliking to you, then you're doing something wrong! As Winston Churchill once famously said – **"You have enemies? Good! That means you stood up for something, sometime in your life!"**

I think of it like this: **If you are pleasing everyone , then there is something seriously wrong!** If your goal in life is to be best friends with everybody on this planet, **then you are never going to be true to yourself and you are never going to be brave enough to stand up for what you believe in.** *Remember what we said about being committed to your principles?* The only way to avoid criticism is to become a spineless people pleaser - and who on earth wants to live life as one of those?!

Here's what I passionately believe: **If you are a genuinely confident and self-assured individual, then you will realise that what other people think of you is none of your business**. You will have the courage to be disliked and you will ensure that your self-esteem is completely independent of other people's opinions! *You will realise that people can think what they like about you, and that you don't have to care!*

It's very clear that when we become dependent on other people's approval and go through life feeling terrified of rejection, we totally lose control over every single area of our lives. When we start taking what other people think about us to heart, we are no longer able to act as autonomous agents. We give up the opportunity to become the very best version of ourselves and instead become slaves to the opinions of people who really do not matter. *How ridiculous is that!*

No matter what other people think about you, you have nothing to worry about. The world will not end just because you are not every single person's flavour of the month!

I know from my own personal experience that people look for validation from other people when they can't find validation within themselves. To escape this desperate search for external validation, it is essential that you stop trying to be liked by everybody and simply decide to just focus on liking yourself!

As long as you are happy and you are not harming anybody else, you've got absolutely nothing to worry about whatsoever! I am a big believer that confidence isn't thinking everyone will like you, it's knowing that you'll be just fine even if they don't. When you become someone who does genuinely like themselves, you realise that whatever anyone else thinks of you, you can handle it. If you find out that someone doesn't particularly like you, you can handle it!

And it's not only that you can handle it – you genuinely should not care about it! You can respect someone's right to having an opinion about you whilst realising that their opinion does not have to affect you in anyway!

Just because one person doesn't like you or like your outfit, it does not mean that the whole world is against you. If someone doesn't like you, it really is nothing personal!

Allow me to share with you these wise words from the inspiring Michelle Obama. She says this:

"You don't have to say anything to the haters. You don't have to acknowledge them at all. You just wake up every morning and be the best that you can be. And that tends to shut them up".

You are here on this planet to fulfil your potential and flourish, not to endlessly worry about what other people think about you.

It is therefore essential for you to remember that **what other people think of you is absolutely none of your business.**

12. IF YOU WOULDN'T TAKE THEIR ADVICE, DON'T LISTEN TO THEIR CRITICISM

" Don't take criticism from someone you wouldn't take advice on" - Ben Wardle

Do not let the opinions of unintelligent, ignorant, rude, and nasty little people get you down. I strongly believe that whilst everybody is entitled to have an opinion about you, under no circumstances do you ever have to pay any attention to this opinion!

When it comes to deciding whether to take what someone thinks about you to heart, you should ask yourself these important questions:

- **Would you turn to these people for life advice or guidance?**

- **Would you trust their opinions on your relationship dilemmas or how to overcome the challenges you were facing in your daily life?**

- **Would you seek out their advice on how to live a good life** and become the best version of yourself?

This is my strong belief: **If you would not trust their advice, then DO NOT listen to their criticisms!** Would you take lessons in loyalty from a serial adulterer? Would you take medical advice about a heart condition from a plumber? Would you take a lesson in quantum physics or the epistemology of religious philosophy from a two-year-old? **Then why are you listening to the opinions of people who have no authority on the subject of your life?**

Do these people even know, care about or have any genuine interest in you? **Are they even forming an opinion about YOU or are they just saying something about the tiny aspect of your identity that they have seen?**

<u>If you do not seek out their advice, then you should never care about their opinion.</u> If you would not seek out their wisdom, then never even *consider* listening to their criticisms!

If you're going to listen to an opinion, then make sure it is coming from an expert!

It is so important to know whose opinions you truly value in life – and listen to these people alone.

This should begin, of course, with your own opinion and how you genuinely feel about yourself. Do you feel that you are living in accordance with your values? Do you make yourself proud and believe you are fulfilling your potential?

Never take criticism from someone you wouldn't take advice from! Who has an important role to play in your life? Who inspires you and guides you? Who genuinely cares for you and wants you to be happy? Who provides you with unconditional acceptance and love? It is your closest family members and your closest friends! It is the people who inspire you and have integrity in your eyes!

Only those in your inner circle have an opinion that is worth listening to. It is only these individuals who can be seen as the 'experts' on you – they are the people who know you, love you and want the best for you.

Every single person is entitled to form an opinion on the tiny bit of you that they see. *It's human nature to make hundreds of split-second judgments and assumptions every single day.*

Human beings are social animals, and so it is only natural for us all to be observing, judging and evaluating the actions of other people.

JS Mil writes this: **"A person who shows rashness, obstinacy, self-conceit - who cannot live within moderate means - who cannot restrain himself from hurtful indulgences - who pursues animal pleasures at the expense of those of feeling and intellect - must expect to be lowered in the opinion of others, and to have a less share of their favourable sentiments; but of this he has no right to complain..."**

You cannot complain about the fact that people have opinions about you! But you also cannot start taking other people's opinions to heart!

The opinions that people form about us are rarely ever accurate. They should therefore never become your sole source of validation in life.

Remember, you should only ever listen to an opinion if it is constructive criticism given to you by an 'expert' (e.g. someone you like, admire, trust and respect)!

What other people think of you is none of your business and absolutely none of your concern! **They are judging a version**

of you that they have seen in the street, not the real you. Focus on what you think of yourself and on becoming the very best version of yourself.

Only take criticism if it is constructive and it is coming from someone who you would turn to for advice.

Remember: most people's judgments of you say more about *them* than they say about the real *you.* You cannot live your life dependent on people making favourable judgements about you – *it is a recipe for disaster and a guaranteed source of endless suffering and discontent.*

So stop trying to be liked by everyone else and start focusing on learning to like yourself instead.

Live your life in accordance with your own values, not at the mercy of other people's uninformed opinions. Take back control, get those earplugs out and stop taking other people's opinions to heart.

It is, of course, essential that we are able to take on board the constructive criticism many people offer to us. Whilst you should never listen to nasty comments and petty remarks, you must always be receptive to constructive criticism from people that you like, trust and admire.

As JS Mill writes, it is essential that human beings help each other to become the best versions of themselves.

He writes this in On Liberty:

"Human beings owe to each other help to distinguish the better from the worse, and encouragement to choose the former and avoid the latter. They should forever be stimulating each other to increased exercise of their higher faculties, and increased direction of their feelings and aims towards wise instead of foolish, elevating instead of degrading, objects and

contemplations".

But he then goes on to add: **"Neither one person, nor any number of persons, is warranted in saying to another creature of ripe years [someone who can think for themselves and make decisions for themselves] that he shall not do with his life for his own benefit what he chooses to do with it".**

In other words, you must at all times remain the absolute soverign of your own life. Other people can advise you, but they can never seek to control or seek to change you. If they aren't trying to help you, then don't pay them any notice whatsoever!

At all times, says Mill, your **"individual spontaneity is entitled to free exercise".** Remember this at all times! People have a right to make whatever judgements about you they like, but you have an equal right to ignore them!

As long as you are not harming anybody else, you are free to do whatever makes you truly happy and fulfilled in life! Other people may advise, suggest, or offer constructive criticism...but at the end of the day, **it is you alone who remains completely responsible for the choices that you make and for the way in which you live your life.**

Remember this at all times: what other people think of you is none of your business! Stop craving validation or approval from irrelevant outsiders! **<u>Never take criticism from somebody you wouldn't take advice from!</u>**

13. ALWAYS REMEMBER THAT YOU ARE ENOUGH

"I exist as I am, that is enough" (Popular Self-Affirmation)

We are all far too critical of ourselves. All too often, we sell ourselves short, put ourselves down and beat ourselves up over the smallest of mistakes. We obsessively worry about what other people think about us and consistently fail to realise just how much potential we have as human beings.

I strongly believe that **the biggest cause of unhappiness in our lives is a feeling of not being good enough.** It is very easy to become paralysed and consumed by the worry that people won't like us, love us or think highly of us.

It is far too easy to become overwhelmed by a fear of failure in every single area of our lives, from our relationships to our careers. It's so easy to start seeing life as one long competition – a competition that we never are never able to win! You seem to always be battling against people who seem to be more confident, popular and attractive than ourselves – you are, in other words, constantly fighting a losing battle!

In order to escape this bottomless pit of insecurity and fear,

we need to start unconditionally accepting ourselves as we authentically are.

Here's what you need to know: **you will never feel fulfilled if you are endlessly chasing other people's approval or forever being driven by a fear of failure. You will be happy with what you've got in the outside world if you are not deeply happy with who you are on the inside first.**

Fulfilment and contentment in life must always come from within. A fulfilling life must always start with fulfilment inside your own soul. So how do we start learning that we are enough? How do we start living genuinely meaningful and fulfilling lives?

I want to introduce you to the life-changing concept of 'Unconditional Self Acceptance', which was first devised by Albert Ellis, a pioneer of contemporary counselling and psychotherapy. The key idea behind USA is extremely simple – it is that **you should unconditionally accept yourself simply because of the fact that you are a unique human being.**

According to Ellis, we need to start telling ourselves this: "I am a person with intentions and choices, as are all humans. As long as I am alive, a member of the human race, and in some ways a unique person, I choose to accept myself unconditionally, whether or not I perform well and whether or not I am approved by others. I prefer to succeed in my projects and I prefer to have other people's approval. But my worth as a person doesn't depend on accomplishment or approbation. It only depends on my choosing to be alive, human and unique".

Let me tell you something important: **the way in which you talk to yourself matters.** Even the most subtle differentiations in our use of language can have a monumental impact on our happiness and self-esteem. For example, there is a big difference between saying to yourself that you would *'prefer'* to be liked and saying to yourself that you *'must'* be liked. It is perfectly normal to 'prefer' certain outcomes – such as preferring to have someone's approval – but it is essential that we never start to believe our entire worth as a human being is totally dependent on one certain outcome. In a nutshell, **It is healthy to prefer a certain outcome, but you should never become dependent on a certain outcome**.

Unconditional Self Acceptance is about knowing that whatever happens in life, you can handle it! **Your worth does not depend on being liked by everyone or never making a mistake – your worth depends solely on the fact that you are alive, you are human, and you are unique!**

If one person does happen to dislike you, then you will obviously be upset and might well feel a little bit hurt. But you should not think that this is the end of the world – **just because you are not one person's cup of tea, that does not mean that you are a complete failure as a human being!** That's because **the only thing that our self-worth should ever depend on is the fact that we are alive.**

At every single moment in your life, you have the choice to unconditionally accept yourself! Here's the Biblical truth that you need to know: **where there is life, there is worth**. And guess what? If you're reading this, you're alive and so you unconditional worth! **Each and every human life is infinitely precious and valuable. Your worth does not depend on your circumstances, your accomplishments or on the approval of others – your worth as a human being is unconditional and comes from deep within you.**

Albert Ellis, the expert psychotherapist, invites us to regularly remind ourselves that "I am a good person simply because I exist, because I am human, because I am a unique individual". *I urge you to repeat this mantra to yourself at every opportunity!* Keep it in mind at all times – **always remember that you have nothing to prove and that there is nobody that you need to impress!** You have intrinsic worth as a human being... simply because you exist!

When we realise that our worth is unconditional, we realise that no matter how much or how little we achieve in life, we are always enough. When we start thinking like this, we give ourselves permission to start living our very best lives. **We give ourselves permission to be unashamedly authentic and to start fearlessly taking risks.**

Knowing that you have unconditional worth allows you escape from the prison of public opinion and escape enslavement to your fears and desires.

With Unconditional Self Acceptance, we know with more confidence than ever before that whatever happens in life, we can handle it! *We start to realise that just because one person doesn't like us or just because one job doesn't quite work out, we are not suddenly failures as human beings!*

It is both absurd and self-defeating to believe that your worth as an individual is dependent on gaining the approval and acceptance of other people. Indeed, Ellis wrote that one of the biggest sources of anxiety in life is this so-called 'ego-overconcern'. This, according to Ellis, is when people become 'terribly afraid that they will do some important task poorly and consequently be disapproved of by others'.

When we care too much about what other people will think about us, we loose all power and control over our lives! **You have to realise that what other people think of you is none of your business! You have to take back control of your self-esteem and your self-worth.**

Your value is not dependent on external approval – as long as you are trying your best to become the best version of yourself, that is more than enough. **As long as you exist as a unique human being, you are enough.**

Therefore, you should know your worth despite what anybody else may say or think. Remember that worth is not a comparison contest and it is not based on how much money you make or how many social media likes you gain. It is not even based on how many friends you have or what grades you got on an exam paper.

Your worth is without question unconditional, and you should therefore unconditionally accept yourself no matter what happens in your life.

It's time to get comfortable in your own skin and start realising that you have absolute and unconditional worth. Give yourself the love and acceptance that every human being deserves – remember at all times that **YOU ARE ENOUGH!**

14. DON'T LET ANYBODY INTIMIDATE YOU

"In life, you only get what you put up with. It is therefore essential that you you become confident at commanding the respect that you deserve" (Ben Wardle)

How often do you catch yourself feeling intimidated by someone you have just me? How frequently do you let rude and arrogant people make you feel small or ruin your day?

Let me tell you something: nothing – and I mean NOTHING – makes my blood boil more than seeing people trying to intimidate other people. I cannot put into words how much rage I feel when I see anybody being bullied, mocked, ridiculed, undermined, or manipulated. I simply cannot STAND IT!

My anger is undoubtedly fuelled by memories of being made to feel so small by people throughout my early life. As the little boy who liked drama and musical theatre, I was always the outsider when it came to being on the playground at school. I always felt - and was made to feel - different from the other children.

As a result of this, I developed an extraordinarily thick skin and protective bubble around myself. I became very just happy doing my own thing and enjoying my own company. I saw it like this: if I wasn't going to get the acceptance or validation from my peers, then I was going to find it from within myself! That independent streak is fiercer today than ever before! As a result of these early experiences of name-calling and exclusion, I became an extraordinarily independent and defensive person. **I told myself that no-one was ever going to make me feel inferior or excluded ever again!**

And this brings me to an important Biblical truth that I today choose to live my life by: <u>**someone can only make you feel intimidated or inferior if you let them.**</u>

It is very clear to us all that every single human being is absolutely equal in value. Nobody is objectively superior or inferior to anyone else in any way whatsoever. At the end of the day, we are all just human beings!

I think that the vast majority of people respect and understand this. They treat other people in the way that they would like to be treated themselves, and they approach other people with a spirit of kindness and friendliness.

There is, however, a sad minority of people who seem to think that they are indeed better than everybody else. As a result of their own insecurities and delusions, they seem to think that it's acceptable to march around putting other people down. Now let's see this appalling behaviour for exactly what it is - these people are desperately trying to make themselves look bigger and more powerful than anyone else in order to cover up their fears and insecurities. They think that the only way of making themselves look bigger is by putting other people down. They foolishly believe that if they convince themselves they are better than everybody else, they will somehow start to feel better about themselves.

Let's get one thing very clear - **you do not have to put up with**

anybody putting you down. Nobody is allowed to make you feel small so that they can feel better about themselves! It's simply not allowed to happen! And so, if you do find yourself feeling undermined, intimidated, or inferior to someone else, you need to remember this: _**you do not have to put up with it!**_

In any situation where you feel like someone is attempting to intimidate you, **You need to take back your control and assert your self-worth.** You need to remember the Biblical truth: <u>**someone can only intimidate you if you let them.**</u> As I alway say, _in life you only get what you put up with!_

Command the respect that you deserve at all times by conducting yourself as a dignified and self-respecting adult. You are not here to be looked down on or treated as if you are inferior – you deserve total respect, and respect is exactly what you are going to get! **When someone intimidates you – intentionally or not – you must stay strong.**

Remember that being intimidated is a choice. Someone can only intimidate you and put you down <u>if you choose to let them</u>. In other words, _make the choice to stop letting people intimidate you and they will then no longer be able to intimidate you!_ Yes - it really is that simple!

Under no circumstances should you ever let yourself feel intimidated. With this in mind, <u>**here is my fool-proof guide to never being intimidated again:**</u>

- IMAGINE THEM NAKED – this is a classic piece of public speaking advice, 'picture everybody in the audience naked'. Now you might find this one a bit traumatising, so don't worry if it doesn't appeal to you! But I find this is a brilliant way of remembering that no matter what someone is wearing –

their outfit, their makeup, etc – they are a human being just like you. Stripped back behind the façade we show the world, we are all just vulnerable human beings. Don't let someone's height, outfit or personal presentation intimidate you. Imagine they've taken off all that makeup and all those clothes – there's nothing special here!

- IMAGINE THEM AS A CHILD AT SCHOOL – just imagine the person back when they were knee-high to a grasshopper! Again, this is a powerful reminder that no matter how big they try and make themselves look they are still deep down just a vulnerable human being like you and I. They were once a tiny little child at primary school who wouldn't hurt a fly – what you're seeing in front of you is all an act and all an attempt to look powerful and important. They're trying to hide that scared and lost child that's within them – see straight through this 'confidence' act and realise they are still that little child arriving at big school for the first time. They're no match for you.

- REMEMBER THAT THEY'RE MORTAL – This person before you is not God. They are not superhuman and they do not have some incredible powers that mean they will live forever. When we are intimidated by someone, we start to believe in their delusions of grandeur. Do yourself a favour and remember that they are just another one of the seven billion human beings on this planet! They were born in the same way as everybody else and they will die in the same way as everybody else. Unless they are quite literally walking on water, don't even think about buying into their God-complex. There's nothing divine about this person in front of you – so don't feed their delusional ego by acting like they're the Lord Jesus Christ!

- IMAGINE THAT YOU ARE THE KING – Well, if you can't beat them you should join them! If they're going to play the 'do you know who I am?' card, then so should you! Join them in their delusions of grandeur – imagine that you are ten times more powerful than they will ever be, and just watch how this changes your body language and self-confidence. I want you to genuinely convince yourself you are ten times more powerful than they could ever be –believe it. You need to take back the power in this situation and remember that someone can only intimidate you if you let them...and you're not going to let them! Make direct eye contact, hold your head up high and signal very clearly that they've picked the wrong person to mess with today. If they think you're going to be made small so they can make themselves feel better, they've got another thing coming!

- SEE THE FUNNY SIDE – Genuinely see the funny side of this insecure idiot thinking they are the King of the World. You've got to be entertained by their delusions of grandeur and their desperation to feel like they're important! I always think of that little Lord Farquaard from Shrek, marching around angrily shouting orders and thinking he was the bees knees. It is actually comedy gold to see someone thinking they're God when in reality they have less power and status than a blade of grass. The more someone tries to prove their importance, the more you realise they have none whatsoever – and you can have a good laugh at the absurd situation before you!

- ASK THEM ABOUT IT – My absolute favourite takedown of all time is to ask someone who clearl thinks they're the Queen 'and who do you think you are?' It is the best way to undermine someone who is secretly insecure and is trying to compensate by acting all-powerful. Make it very clear you are not impressed by their apparent status in the slightest – unless you are face to face with God Himself, then you should act disinterested and unimpressed by anyone acting like they are the Creator of the Heavens and Earth. By asking them who they think they are, you make it very clear that you are not buying this bullshit and you will not be intimidated. Whilst most people will start kissing this delusional person's feet, you are refusing to bow down to their delusions. Ask them this question and you will powerfully undermine them…leave them lost for words and desperately struggling to take back their self-made crown!

In summary, remember that somebody is only ever able to intimidate you if you let them! This is why it is so important for you to know your worth at all

Nobody has any right whatsoever to make you feel intimidated, undermined, or inferior - and they are only be able to make you feel like this if you let them! Remember that you only ever get what you put up with in life – and you are not going to put up with somebody putting you down! No one has more human rights than you and no one has a right to try and make you feel inferior to them in any way.

Stand up for yourself, keep your worth at the very forefront of your mind…and REFUSE TO BE INTIMIDATED BY ANYBODY!

Never let some insecure idiot with a God-complex try to put you down or ruin your day. **If someone is ever trying to put**

you down, don't you dare put up with it!

15. YOUR ATTITUDE IS EVERYTHING

"Everything can be taken from a man but one thing: the last of the human freedoms – to choose one's attitude in any given set of circumstances, to choose one's own way". (Viktor Frankl, Auschwitz Concentration Camp survivor)

Take responsibility for your attitude towards life! I cannot emphasise how important this is! Take control of your life before life takes control of you! You are the master of your own destiny!

We have within us all of the resources required in order to transform our lives and turn every single one of our dreams into our new reality. Realise this: you have the potential to achieve all of your dreams, to overcome all of your fears and to become the very best version of yourself.

Only one thing is required: a Positive Mental Attitude! With a positive attitude we are able to develop an unshakeable commitment to becoming the very best version of ourselves in every single situation that we face in our lives! We realise that whatever happens in our lives, we can handle it!

So many of us go through life with a 'victim mindset'. We

waste so much of our precious time and energy complaining about things that have happened to us. We blame other people for our unhappiness and tell anyone who will listen to us that life isn't fair! We feel sorry for ourselves and angry with the world, working ourselves up and wishing that things could be different.

I used to be a very sensitive soul, and I used to think with a real 'victim mindset' about the homophobic comments that I would regularly receive. In my head, I started to believe that the whole world was against me and that all anybody ever saw when they looked at me was 'GAY'. Because of the comments being made about me, I started to believe that I would never be accepted, that I would never be successful and that I would never find happiness in my life as a result. I felt so bitter about the fact that everywhere I went, people would stare at me and make comments about me. I had a real chip on my shoulder about the fact that whilst so many people were seemingly able to just breeze through life, I was being knocked down and laughed at every single day! I well and truly saw myself as a victim of other people's opinions.

But one day, I remember stopping myself dead in my tracks and asking myself - *where exactly is this attitude towards life actually getting you? Why am I living my whole life as a victim of other people's opinions? Why am I letting other people label and define me? Why on earth am I giving these nasty, rude and irrelevant people so much power?*

I started to realise exactly what I needed to do – **I needed to take back control of my life!** I realised that I needed to stop listening to my victim narrative and choose instead to become the master of my own destiny. And this began with **taking complete responsibility for my attitude towards life.**

Today, I wholeheartedly choose to embrace - and in fact use

to my advantage - the fact that people take one look at me and label me as 'gay'. I make no secret of the fact that I shamelessly play up to the stereotypes people impose on me... and indeed use these stereotypes to my advantage! I don't think twice before totally 'playing up' to the caricature people have of me in their heads!

 use these stereotypes and prejudices to my advantage, safe in the knowledge that my closest friends and family know the 'real' me. They know that my identity is not just being 'GAY' or 'not a typical boy'. They instead unconditionally accept me as a human being – they love me for being the multi-layered, three dimensional and REAL person that I am!

I absolutely love it when people assume that I'm studying fashion or drama at University - both excellent degrees to be studying, by the way. I love seeing the shock on people's faces when I reveal that I am actually studying religion, philosophy and ethics! **Underestimate me at your peril, I like to think, because whilst you're busy putting me in a box and defining me by my sexuality, I'm busy using my brain and getting ahead in life!**

I think this is a *very* good example of how changing your attitude means that you can turn a source of suffering in your life into a catalyst for success. **You can take back the power over your life and become the author of your next chapter!**

It really is time for a news flash (just call me Fiona Bruce!) - **no matter how you are feeling in life right now, things CAN be different!** You do not have to be a victim for the rest of your life. You do not have to let other people's opinions get you down and you do not have to be defined by the expectations and judgements imposed on you by society!

We live in a world that is obsessed with putting people into boxes. Well I'm sorry, but if you think that I'll be spending the rest of my life stuck inside someone else's box, you can think again! This is what I passionately believe: **We must start to realise the very clear difference between the things over which we have full control and the things over which we have no control whatsoever. <u>And we must realise that the only thing over which we will ever have complete control is ourselves.</u>**

More specifically, **<u>the only thing that we have complete control over is our attitude towards life.</u>** There is absolutely no point worrying or getting angry about the things over which we have no control – **if you can't do anything about it, then don't waste your precious energy worrying about it!**

Here's what I strongly believe: **What matters is not what has happened to you but how you have chosen to respond.** We can't get angry or frustrated about things over which we have no control (e.g. what has happened to you) - we have to simply accept what has happened and then choose to respond in the most intelligent and dignified way that we can.

Allow me to illustrate this with a little weather-themed example! Imagine that you were planning to go on a lovely little coastal walk, and that you were hoping it would be a gloriously sunny day. But here's the problem - you've just looked out of the window and seen that it is absolutely pouring it down with rain.

What do you do in this situation? Do you spend the day sitting on your bed and wishing it was sunny? Do you scream at the clouds and tell them to go away? We know that this will achieve absolutely nothing at all other than cause us even greater anger and harm! Or do you accept the reality, get on your raincoat and wellies...and stoically head out for your walk regardless? Do you hide away in the house or do you decide to fully embrace this challenge?

Whatever the situation that you find yourself in, you must always bravely accept your fate and stoically resolve to make the best of it!

You can still make the most of your day, even if the weather - over which you have absolutely no control whatsoever - isn't in your favour. You can still make a success of your life by focusing on what you can control (your attitude) instead of getting angered and upset about things you cannot (everything else).

In 1946, the incredibly inspiring Holocaust survivor Viktor Frankl first published his autobiography 'Man's Search for Meaning', in which he describes his horrifying experiences as a prisoner in the Nazi Concentration Camp Auschwitz.

He describes the unfathomably cruel torture inflicted on men, women and children by the Nazis in charge of running these horrific death camps. He writes: **"Everything can be taken from a man but one thing: the last of the human freedoms – to choose one's attitude in any given set of circumstances, to choose one's own way".**

Writing about his horrific treatment at the hands of camp commanders, Frankl explains: **"The experiences of camp life show that man does have a choice of action...Man can preserve a vestige of spiritual freedom, of independence of mind, even in such terrible conditions of psychic and physical stress".**

At every hour of every day in the camp, Frankl said that the prisoners had **"the opportunity to make a decision, a decision which determined whether you would submit to those powers which threatened to rob you of your very self, your inner freedom; which determined whether or not you would** become the plaything of circumstance, renouncing freedom and dignity to become moulded into the form of the typical inmate".

The millions of people who were held in Nazi concentration camps and subjected to the most inhumane treatment had *almost* all of their autonomy taken away from them.

I say *almost*, because what remained fully within their power was the attitude and mindset that they chose. **They could choose, despite their horrific circumstances, to preserve their 'spiritual freedom' and 'independence of mind'.**

This was something that the Nazi camp commanders never had for themselves – they had sold their souls to the devil and had consented to becoming instruments in Hitler's horrific genocide.

At the core of Frankl's philosophy is **the idea that every individual has the freedom to change at every instant**. He believed that **we all have the capacity to rise above our current conditions - whatever they may be - and to grow beyond them.** Frankl writes: **'I bear witness to the unexpected extent to which man is capable of defying and braving even the worst conditions conceivable'.**

No matter what has happened to us or how we have been treated by others, **we are always capable of choosing to make the world a better place. We are always capable of fulfilling our potential as meaning-seeking human beings.**

In our 21st century lives, there are so many things that we simply can't control. It might be something as trivial as the weather, or it could be a social factor such as other people's opinions. We have to accept that we cannot do anything about these things – remember the Stoic notion of 'amor fati'? Instead, **we must commit ourselves to choosing our attitude**

and taking full responsibility for the mindset that we maintain. We are then capable of taking complete ownership of our responses to the situations in which we find ourselves.

It is so important to realise that you are not a victim of life but the master of your own destiny! Focus wholeheartedly on the things over which you do have full control (your own attitude and actions) and learn to simply accept the things which you can do absolutely nothing about (everything else).

It's time to take control of your life! Focus all of your time, effort, and energy on the things over which you *do* have full control and autonomy. **Seize every opportunity to become the author of your next chapter and the master of your own mindset.**

You have the potential to become the best version of yourself, no matter what circumstances or situations you find yourself in.

All that is required is for you to take responsibility for your attitude towards life, and commit to becoming the master of your own destiny.

The power really is in your own very hands...

16. STOP UNDERESTIMATING YOURSELF!

"You're probably overestimating what's going against you, and underestimating what is within you" (Brianna Wiest)

Abraham Maslow once said that 'the story of the human race is the story of men and women selling themselves short'.

The modern epidemic of low self-esteem is a real 21st century crisis. Too many people allow their doubts and fears to place limitations on their lives. They exist only within the boundaries of their comfort zones, convinced that success doesn't come easily to people like them. Well success certainly isn't going to come to you if you don't believe you're capable of it!

Underestimating yourself is a shocking act of self-sabotage. As a result of our tendency to underestimate ourselves, so many of us never manage to fulfil our purpose as human beings. Instead of flourishing through life, we are instead driven by feelings of fear and anxiety.

When we let our fears, worries, and insecurities take over our lives, we turn our lives into a self-fulfilling prophecy of suffering! When we underestimate ourselves, we fail to realise our potential and end up condemning ourselves to a life of disappointment and unhappiness! **We therefore need to become**

vigilant against this tendency to underestimate ourselves!

Our biggest fear as human beings is our fear of not being good enough. This fear seems to drive all of the other fears that we experience as human beings – our fears of rejection or confrontation, for example. When we get caught up in the 'I'm not good enough' mentality, we are failing to remember the golden rule that **'whatever happens in life, you can handle it'.**

In order to fight back against the 'I'm not good enough' mentality, **we need to remember that our worth as human beings is unconditional, and that our value as a human being is not dependent on the approval of other people.** We need to stop underestimating ourselves and start realising our full potential instead!

Here's a question for you - What is it that sets the top-performing athletes, politicians, entertainers, and business leaders apart from everybody else? What do the top 1% of achievers have that the other 99% are lacking? **The answer? It is a spirit of self-confidence and resilience!**

Here's what I believe: **To get to the top, you need to believe that you can get to the top!** *In other words, you need to stop underestimating yourself!*

If you don't believe in yourself, then what hope in hell is there that anybody else is going to believe in you either? If you don't think that you should get the job, then what chance is there that the person interviewing you for it will think you should either? **If you don't have confidence in your own capabilities, then nobody else is going to have confidence in your capabilities either!**

In order to turn your dreams into our reality, you have to

believe that you can do it! We need to stop underestimating ourselves and start realising our full potential as independent and autonomous human beings!

All that this requires is two very simple things – self-confidence and resilience. We need the self-confidence to know that we can achieve our dreams, and we need the resilience to know that if we encounter any challenge or obstacles, we will be able to overcome them.

In short: in order to achieve success in your life, you need to stop underestimating yourself and start believing in yourself instead!

Brian Tracy once wrote this: **"The potential of the average person is like a huge ocean unsailed, a new continent unexplored, a world of possibilities waiting to be released and channeled toward some great good".**

You need to know that you can fulfill all of your dreams and achieve all of your goals. **Realise that within you, you have the strength and resilience to bounce back from every single setback that you may face in your life!** Make sure that you remember our golden rule - whatever happens in your life, you can handle it!

I cannot stress this to you enough – **if you fail to see your own potential, then you cannot complain when other people can't see your potential either!** You need to believe that you **can** pass that exam and that you **can** shine in that job interview. **It's time to realise that you are indeed good enough and that you are capable of achieving all of your life goals...and more!**

Now, that's not to say that you've got to become arrogant and totally delusional about your own self-importance. Delusions of grandeur and unchecked egos help absolutely nobody! But what you do need is a real sense of self-confidence and a real commitment to being resilient.

Know that you are capable of achieving a lot more than you think – if you can dream it, you can achieve it! All that you need to get there is self-confidence, hard work and resilience!

So what are you waiting for? Let's roll up our sleeves, start putting ourselves out there... and **never underestimate ourselves again!**

17. STAND UP FOR YOURSELF

"Develop enough courage so that you can stand up for yourself and then stand up for somebody else" (Maya Angelou)

I hate to break it to you, but this planet is not populated with clones of Mother Teresa! I don't like to burst your bubble, but not every single person on the face of the earth is a saint! It's a brutal fact of life that the vast majority of people on this planet are in it for themselves. It is a jungle out there and people will not think twice before walking all over you and using you to get exactly what they want.

The reality of life is this: **if you don't stand up for yourself, you are going to end up getting used, abused and walked all over.** As the 16th century philosopher Thomas Hobbes observed, the life of man is a real "war of all against all". As Charles Darwin realised, the human condition can be best described as 'survival of the fittest'. People are naturally self-interested and so will do whatever it takes - at whatever cost to other people - in order to protect themselves and gain more power for themselves. And so if **we do not assert ourselves and command the respect that we deserve, we are highly likely to be eaten alive!** It really is a jungle out there, and **if you don't stand up for yourself and actively protect yourself from harm, you will not survive in our society.**

If you give most people an inch, they really will take a mile... and more! It's a sad fact of life that many people in our world today see other people as resources that they can use in order to fulfil their selfish needs and desires. They don't think twice before using someone for sex or becoming friends with someone solely for the sake of enhancing their own social status.

Instead of wanting to genuinely connect with you as a human being, there are so many people who simply want to get something out of you. And once they've got what they want, they will see no problem with simply discarding and abandoning you. You have served your purpose and fulfilled their needs, and so you no longer have any worth in their eyes.

This is completely unacceptable. No human being deserves to be treated as if they were some kind of disposable product. Nobody deserves to ever be treated like a piece of meat that can be thrown away once it's past it's sell-by date. Remember the 'non-harm principle' from John Stuart Mill? Humans are free to do whatever makes them genuinely happy, as long as they are not causing harm to other people in the process. Now whilst it would be wonderful for everyone in the world to follow this principle, the reality of human life is that many people obviously do not. And so if you don't stand up for yourself and assert your power as a human being, people will not think twice before causing you harm - they will manipulate, exploit you, and use you for their own personal gain without a single drop of sympathy, empathy or guilt.

That is why you need to toughen up. You need to stop bending over backwards for people who would not think twice before throwing you under a bus. You need to realise that you are not just an object of sexual desire, the provider of a service, or the fulfilment of a need.

As the 18th century philosopher Immanuel Kant wrote, 'al-

ways treat human beings as an end in themselves, never simply as a mean to an end'. This means that human beings should be respected as autonomous individuals, rather than being used and exploited for the selfish gain of others.

You need to start realising **you only ever get what you put up with**. People will only be able to walk all over you <u>if you let them</u>. And the guaranteed way of stopping people from taking you for a fool is knowing how to confidently and assertively stand up for yourself!

Standing up for yourself begins with the realisation that you are an empowered human being who deserves to be treated with absolute respect. If you do not realise that you deserve respect - and then actively command this respect - then I'm sorry but you cannot be surprised when people don't treat you with respect!

You need to remember this: **you are not just a topic of conversation, an object of sexual attraction or the fulfilment of a need ...you are a human being!** You are a human being with a brain! You therefore need to start using that brain and realise that if you don't start stand ing up for yourself, people will continue walking all over you.

The fact of the matter is this: if you give some people that inch, they will not think twice before trying to take a mile-. **If you fail to be assertive in knowing your worth and commanding the respect you deserve, then but you cannot be surprised when people start walking all over you!** To put it another way, if you do not actively command the respect that you deserve in life, then you cannot complain when you end up getting used by other people.

Here's an everyday example; imagine you go for coffee with a friend every Sunday at 11am. Except they are never there at 11am. Every week, they arrive 10 minutes late, 30 minutes late – some weeks they turn up an hour late! What's worse, they don't even seem to feel bad about it whatsoever – 'oh you know what I'm like' they exclaim as they turn up at 1.30pm. They don't seem to realise, or perhaps don't even care, that you have a life. It's all about them and unless you assert your worth, it will continue to always be all about them. They know you're not going to say anything so they walk all over you – they make no effort to turn up on time because you've never had the backbone to say something about it the past 100 times they have been late! You give them that inch and they take a mile.

Let's keep it real - you do not deserve to be sat there waiting hours for them to turn up. It is rude, disrespectful and shows a total disregard for your time. This so-called friend is blatantly failing to respect you and, unless you make it clear that you expect to be respected, they'll clearly think that they can continue to walk all over you. This is a very simple example, but the principles can be applied in all areas of our lives.

The fact of the matter is this: **in life, you only get what you put up with.** That is why you need to start standing up for yourself. You need to know your worth and command the respect that you deserve. If you don't want people to keep walking all over you, then you need to stop acting like a door mat!

People need to know how you expect to be treated and what kind of treatment you are absolutely not prepared to put up with! You need to have strong boundaries in place and have the self-confidence to know when it is time to walk away (with, of course, your head held high). **You do not have to**

suffer as someone else's 'means to an end'. Remember, **You deserve to be treated with absolute respect!**

You need to start standing up for yourself, because nobody else is going to do it for you!

Remember, you are the master of your own destiny and you have to take full responsibility for every single area of your life! This includes the way in which other people treat you , because you are totally responsible for setting the tone for how other people treat you.

Always stand up for yourself - you are worth standing up for.

With this in mind, here are my 4 top tips on standing up for yourself in everyday life:

•   **Be clear about your boundaries.** Know what you will and will not tolerate. Don't make excuses or allowances for people who fail to treat you with respect – know what kind of behaviour you are prepared to put up with. When someone crosses the line, do not feel bad in walking away from them with your head held high. If you don't, they will keep walking all over you. If you give someone an inch they will take a mile. Of course, it is always possible to make amends and start afresh! But you must be very clear about what you will and will not put up with – you owe it to yourself to have explicit boundaries…and to stick to them! They will protect you from being exploited and stop you from being used to fulfil someone else's selfish needs.

•   **Be assertive in your conversations.** Stop being scared of saying no! If you do not want to do something or are not happy with someone's behaviour, then you need to say it! This will earn you ten million times more respect than bending over backwards and becoming known as a 'yes' person! You have a voice and you have an opinion – it is essential that you calmly and clearly express it as part of conversation. This is one of my strongest beliefs in life: **don't signal it, say it**! Don't hope someone will 'get the message' – spell it out for them! Not only does this ensure that your voice is heard, but it also stops you storing up anger and frustration that will cause even greater problems further down the line! It is so dangerous to start playing emotional games or to start hoping that someone will 'just realise' that they've upset you! If you don't spell it out, they'll never know! The more you bottle things up, the more trouble you store up for later on. Start being more assertive about how you feel and where you stand on a subject, and start commanding the respect that you deserve!

• **Don't be scared to walk away.** In the same way that you should never be scared of saying no, you should never be scared of walking away from a situation that isn't serving you. If you are in a toxic friendship or relationship, it is absolutely essential that you are able to walk away. You are not dependent on anyone – you will survive without them! The moment you become utterly dependent on someone is the moment you lose all of your individual autonomy, power and self-respect. Know that you can survive without them, and so you do not have to just put up with anything they throw at you. Remember, only stick around as long as something is serving you. If they cross the line, you have to walk away. Don't worry about losing people in your life. Whatever happens you can handle it – so make sure you always choose dignity over desperation. You are not desperate for friends! It is more important to like yourself than be liked by everybody else. Standing up for yourself means being brave enough to walk away from any relationship or situation that isn't serving you in positive ways.

• **Believe in your cause.** Believing in yourself is the most important foundation for becoming a confident and competent human being. If you doubt your worth or doubt the purpose behind what you're doing, then you become someone who is very easy to manipulate and coerce. People will sense this moral weakness and exploit it – if people know you are insecure and impressionable, they know that they can use you to their advantage and get whatever it is that they want out of you. In order to stop this from happening, you need to be very clear about your purpose in life and assertively live in accordance with your moral principles. It is essential that you KNOW YOUR WORTH! Know the answer to these questions: What is the purpose of your life? What is it that you want out of this situation?

What do you want to achieve? What kind of person do you want to be? Most importantly, what are the core values that are driving you in life? Without strong moral foundations, we are easy to mould.

If you don't know what you believe and what you truly value in life, you will spend your life being used by other people who want to exploit your lack of self-confidence for their own selfish gain.

Be very clear about knowing your worth and believing in your cause – assert yourself as an empowered, informed and autonomous individual!

18. STOP HOLDING BACK

"Stop holding back and make a move. The future belongs to the 'risk-takers' not the 'comfort seekers'" (Brian Tracy)

Life is not a dress rehearsal. You are not doing a quick 'walk-through' of how it all works before you get started with the real deal. **This lifetime that you are experiencing right now is the only one that you will ever have.** There are no second chances and there is never going to be an opportunity to go all the way back to the start.

As a result, you have absolutely no choice but to seize the day and live every second of your life to the absolute full. Realising that life is so finite and precious should be a real wake up call to every single one of us.

Life is short - and so we need to stop holding back and instead start living every single day to the full. The fact of the matter is this: You really do not know which day is going to be your last . *What guarantee is there that you are actually going to wake up tomorrow morning?*

The truth is that there is absolutely NONE - there is never ***any*** guarantee that we will get to experience even just one more day day on this planet! And so we therefore need to get serious about living every second of our precious lives to the absolute full!

With this in mind, I want you to ask yourself this – **in what areas of my life am I holding back right now?** It might be:

- You're holding back part of your personality/identity because you're scared of rejection.

- You're holding back on telling people what you really want or how you feel because you don't think anyone will listen or that your voice isn't valid.

- You're holding back from doing the things in life that truly make you happy because you're scared of what people will say/think

- You're holding back from telling someone you love them because you're scared of being rejected or embarrassed.

- You're holding back from starting a conversation with someone you'd like to get to know because you don't know how they're going to react – you're scared they'll laugh in your face

- You're holding back from pursuing your dream job because you don't believe that you're good enough

- You're holding back from being unashamedly authentic in your life because you're scared of losing the support of loved ones

In my own life, a fear of being embarrassed and being laughed at have led to me holding myself back time and time again. My fears have felt like impenetrable barriers that I could never seem to move beyond. But as a result of my hospitalisation with anorexia, I started to realise just how fragile and precious human life really was. I woke up to the fact that you really do not know when your last day on this earth will be.

I realised that our days really are numbered - the clock is ticking, and we cannot afford to waste one single moment of our precious time here on this planet!

As I've grown older, I've started to realise that if I don't start working hard to overcome my fears, **I will end up lying on my death bed bitterly regretting not living my life to the full.**

Why, I would be asking myself as I lay there taking my last breaths, had I imposed limitations on my life because of an irrational fear what some irrelevant person might think of me? Why had I wasted so much of my precious time worrying about irrelevant people's utterly irrelevant opinions?

After reflecting on the preciousness of human life, I realised that is absolutely no excuse for not seizing every single day as another opportunity to become the best version of yourself!

As the motivational speaker Tony Robbins once said, **if you want to make it big, then you have got to push yourself beyond your limits.**

Here's what you need to know: **You cannot live your life paralysed by a fear of other people's opinions. You cannot live your life paralysed by a crippling anxiety about what could go wrong.**

Your life is too short to be anything but fearlessly authentic! So stop holding back and start living every single second of your life to the full!

I challenge you to seize every single day that you have on this planet, and I urge you to become fearless about putting yourself out there in the world! Stop being paralysed by your fears and start chasing your dreams. Become fearless about stepping outside of your comfort zone!

Over the past few years, I've made it my personal mission to stop holding back and to start living my life to the very full.

I went for Head Boy at Sixth Form and got it, I started a YouTube channel, moved to London for university, got a job at Europe's biggest LGBT+ nightclub, started a TikTok account featuring me being my absolutely authentic self and, of course, started writing this little book of essays! I've also found to courage to put myself to get out there on the dating scene, allowing me to overcome my longstanding fear of rejection and challenge my deep rooted anxiety about not being attractive enough to catch anyone's eye.

There's still so much that I want to do, but I am so proud of how many fears I have already conquered, and so proud of how many risks I have already been brave enough to take. If I can do all of this, then so can you!

Based on my experiences so far in life, I can tell you with confidence that it's time for you to get fearless about living your life to the full!

 It's time for you to realise your limitless potential and stop letting your fears, worries and anxieties get in your way.

As William James once wrote: **"I have no doubt whatsoever that most people live - whether physically, intellectually or morally - in a very restricted circle of their potential being...we all have reservoirs of life to draw upon of which we do not dream".**

It is time to start dreaming big and it is time to start fearlessly living our very best lives! Escape your restricted circle and live your life to the full.

This lifetime is your time to shine - so stop holding back and start living your best life!

19. CHALLENGE YOUR IRRATIONAL BELIEFS

"The best years of your life are the ones in which you decide your problems are your own. You do not blame them on your mother, the ecology or the president. You realise that you control your own destiny" (Albert Ellis)

How often do you outsource responsibility for your problems to other people? How frequently do you find yourself blaming external circumstances for your unhappiness in life?

It's very easy for human beings to slip into what I call the 'victim mindset', which is a way of thinking where we believe that the world is against us and there's absolutely nothing we can do about it (other than feel sorry for ourselves).

This mindset is the most toxic place we could ever be. It is a bleak destination of total helplessness and despair! This is because when you start to believe that you are a victim of the universe, you give up any power, control and autonomy you ever had over your life.

As I always say, **in order to start living your best life you need to get serious about becoming the master of your own destiny! And this all begins by taking full control of your own mind!**

So what is the secret to digging yourself out of the dangerous victim mindset? How can you get yourself back on the path to happiness and empowerment?

Your journey to taking back control of your life begins with one key realisation - that **your Mindset and Beliefs Matter**!

Allow me to explain. Your beliefs about events that happen matter more than the events themselves. **The lens through which you see the world completely shapes your whole experience of life.** As the pioneering psychotherapist Albert Ellis once wrote, **"People and things do not upset us. Rather, we upset ourselves by believing that they can upset us".** At the core of Albert Ellis' life-changing philosophy is the idea that your beliefs are completely responsible for shaping your behaviours and therefore defining your life.

Remember, it is not the events themselves but your beliefs about these events that shape your experience of life! **Our beliefs drive us, shape us and influence us more than anything else. What you think and believe, you become.**

Here's the thing about human beings: We are all constantly existing in a cycle of 'thoughts, feelings and behaviours'. We are all acting on autopilot and responding impulsively to things that happen in our lives . **This is why it is so important that the beliefs you hold are rational.**

What do we mean by a 'rational belief'? According to Ellis, there are two different kinds of belief that human beings tend to hold - beliefs are either rational and irrational. Rational Beliefs are beliefs that are flexible, non-extreme and logical. For example, 'I would love to succeed but I don't have to' or 'If people are rude to me I will not be happy about it, but I can survive it'. Irrational belief are beliefs that are rigid, extreme and illogical. For example, 'If I don't succeed in my presentation life will be ruined!' or 'If people are rude to me I cannot stand it!'

In order to live a happy life, we need to challenge any irrational beliefs we might be holding onto and replace them with more rational ones. Whilst irrational beliefs are demanding and tend to catastrophise situations, rational beliefs help us to make sense of the world in a reasonable and healthy way.

Rational beliefs express preferences - rather than demands - about what we would like to happen in our lives. When we are thinking rationally, we know what we would prefer to be the outcome of a certain situation, but we also know that oue life does not depend on this outcome.

Can you identify any irrational beliefs that are driving your behaviours and potentially contributing to any feelings of anxiety, despair or frustration in life?

I saw first-hand the effects of living a life held hostage to Irrational Beliefs when I was hospitalised with the eating disorder anorexia aged just 12. This mental health condition had taken full control over my life – anorexic thoughts and beliefs drove me to almost starve myself to death, culminating with my hospitalisation in the autumn of 2013. I had been totally and utterly consumed by these anorexic beliefs, which led to months of shockingly disordered eating and the worst body image issues imaginable.

To the outside world, I was becoming skin and bones – a shell of my former self in both personality and physical appearance. Within my own head, where anorexic beliefs had totally taken over, I was unable to think about anything other than losing more weight and believing that food was my absolute enemy. As my body became weaker, the anorexic beliefs became stronger – all of my thoughts were only ever about weight, food, calories and control.

In the end, I was hospitalised by doctors who would later tell me that if had not taken such decisive action, I would have undoubtedly have starved myself to death. I vividly remember a consultant paediatrician asking me directly, 'Is that what you want Ben? Do you want to die?'

Up until this moment, I had been in total self-destruct mode. Everyone around me had known that there was something seriously wrong – just one look at me would have shown anyone that I was seriously ill and in need of urgent medical help. But in my own head, I was completely and utterly in denial. I would angrily refuse to listen to my concerned parents and despite people's concerns remained desperately intent on losing even more weight and finding out how much more I could restrict the number of calories that I was consuming.

It really is a miracle that I survived my battle with anorexia. Irrational beliefs had completely and utterly taken over my life. My organs were failing and my body was collapsing. I had absolutely no energy and was providing myself with absolutely no nutrition whatsoever. *All that I can think now is this - thank God that the medical professionals intervened and acted so decisively when they did!*

After several weeks under twenty-four-hour observation in hospital, the doctors deemed me well enough to be discharged from the ward. This would just be the very beginning of a long road to recovery. When I look back on this experience, I find myself asking 101 different questions about what on earth was going on. Was I really so unhappy that I was prepared to starve myself to death? How on earth did my mental wellbeing spiral to such a shockingly low level?

As I lay their in my hospital bed, I remember suddenly coming to this realisation that life was too precious to be ruined by irrational beliefs. Almost overnight, I realised that I could not afford to spend another single moment of my life as a victim of these irrational anorexic thoughts!

So when I was finally allowed to return home and my therapy sessions began, I became genuinely committed to getting better. I couldn't afford to risk my life like that again! I no longer wanted my whole life to revolve around weight loss, calories and those anorexic thoughts – instead, I genuinely wanted to be happy. I didn't want to continue living a life of starvation and self-hatred - I wanted to live a life of flourishing and fulfillment! And I wanted to inspire others who might have been in that same dark place as me – I wanted to show those suffering from this horrific mental illness that there was a light at the end of the tunnel. I wanted to continue transmitting my core message - 'If I can do it, then so can you!'

How was I going to take back that control of my life and banish those anorexic thoughts for good? My CBT therapist taught me to start identifying the thoughts and beliefs that were driving my feelings and behaviours. She taught me to ask myself 'What is motivating these anorexic behaviours? What is the reason for my obsession with waistline, calories and control?'

I started to consider different possible answers - Could it have been the bullying I had received for being 'gay' (based on my mannerisms and the assumptions people made about me – I was literally 11 years old), or could it have been the feeling I never quite fit in anywhere at school? Perhaps I was sick of people labelling me as 'gay' and wanted to take back some control in my life? Maybe I believed that there was a correlation between weight loss and happiness, and that by punishing myself in this way I would be able to escape my feelings of low self-esteem and loneliness?

It is incredible how much CBT taught me about the power of our thoughts, feelings, and beliefs. By cultivating a real insight into the workings of my own mind, I was able to learn how to take back control of my own thoughts and beliefs. As a result, I was finally in a position to start disputing and challenging the anorexic thoughts that were driving my shockingly disordered eating habits and behaviours.

After so many months of starvation, self-punishment and self-destructive behaviours, I remember feeling so liberated and overjoyed to finally be getting my life back! I loved the fact that I was actually able to think rationally again! I was delighted that I was now able to think about something other than weight loss and calories! I now even had the energy to smile, to laugh, and to do some of the things that I loved again!

When you learn to start challenging your irrational beliefs, you are able to get back in the driving seat of your own life. Perhaps most importantly, you are finally strong yourself to give yourself that essential love and self-compassion we all so desperately need!

Learning to challenge my irrational beliefs enabled me to finally take back control from my eating disorder. When you take back control of your mind, the anorexic beliefs don't get to rule over your life anymore...YOU do! You start to realise that your life is not defined by weight, calories, and body image. You start to realise that it is completely irrational to keep punishing yourself through a gruelling and abusive programme of self-hatred, starvation and pain.

As I got stronger and stronger, I started to realise the shocking extent to which I had become a victim of my own irrational beliefs!

I was finally learning how to stop listening to the negative narrative in my mind and to start searching for 'evidence' that might actually support the beliefs that I was holding. Instead of just believing that 'nobody likes me', for example, it became my homework to find evidence that would actually support this belief. It was my task to keep asking myself: what evidence do I actually have to support this belief? Is there any empirically-based proof that this belief is true? **I started to realise that my anorexic beliefs were totally irrational and supported by no credible evidence whatsoever!**

Like a scientist studying in the lab, **CBT teaches us to become students of our own minds.** It teaches us to become experts at observing our own thoughts and to become confident at identifying and challenging any irrational beliefs that might be driving our behaviours! As I continued on my road to recovery, I became convinced that learning to challenge my irrational beliefs through Cognitive Behavioural Therapy had saved my life. The doctors in hospital had told me that I was quite literally starving myself to death – my blood pressure, heart rate and the functioning of my essential organs were dangerously bad. If I had not been hospitalised, it would only have been a matter of time before my body had completely given up. As a result of anorexia, I would have been dead before my 13th birthday.

Looking back, I can see now that those anorexic thoughts were not going to stop for anything or anybody. If I hadn't have been hospitalised, I would undoubtedly have ended up starving myself to death. My life was saved by the medical professionals at the hospital, to whom I will forever be grateful. And

I was given a brand new life by the therapist who introduced me to Cognitive Behavioural Therapy, which liberated me from my anorexic thoughts and enabled me to break free from the destructive beliefs that were ruining – and on the verge of ending – my life.

Here's the key thing that I learned – **you must protect yourself from irrational beliefs!** Don't get complacent about the beliefs you allow to take root in your mind! Make sure you challenge them, question them, and evaluate them! Ask yourself, **Is what I am thinking about this situation a true reflection of reality?** Do I have **evidence for what I am thinking about this person, or am I being driven by irrational feelings of anxiety and insecurity?** As you go through life, you must make sure that you are continuously challenging and evaluating your beliefs. Question whether they are rational and ensure that they are helping you to become the best version of yourself.

Because if a belief isn't helping you become the best version of yourself, then what purpose is it actually serving in your head? And if all that a belief is fuelling negative feelings of self-doubt and insecurity, then why are you still holding onto it?

Here's what I know for sure - **If you don't take responsibility for your thoughts and beliefs, they will take over and ruin your whole life.**

That is why I urge you: don't run the risk of letting your irrational beliefs take over and destroy your whole entire life! Remember, **it's not events themselves that cause happiness or harm – it's our interpretations of them.**

As I always like to say, the power is in your own hands – seize this opportunity to take ownership of your life and become the master of your own mind! You deserve to live a genuinely happy and fulfilling life, and that begins with becoming the vigilant observer and intelligent manager of your own thoughts and beliefs!

Let me share with you something that the Stoic philosopher and Roman Emperor Marcus Aurelius wrote in his book of Meditations:

"Revere your power of judgement. All rests on this to make sure that your directing mind no longer entertains any judgement which fails to agree with the nature or the constitution of a rational being. And this state guarantees deliberate thought, affinity with other men, and obedience to the gods".

What you think you become - and you owe it to yourself to become the best version of yourself! **Escape from the prison of your irrational thoughts and beliefs - and give yourself the permission to live a genuinely happy, enriching and fulfilling life!**

20. MAKE FULFILLMENT YOUR FOCUS

"Happiness is a state of inner fulfilment, not the gratification of inexhaustible desires for outward things" (Matthieu Ricard)

None of us should be satisfied with 'just surviving' in life. Man cannot live on bread alone – it is not sufficient to go through life just fulfilling your basic needs for food, shelter, and sex! Instead of being satisfied with just surviving through each day, you should make it your mission to absolutely thrive through life as the best possible version of yourself.

As you know, I passionately believe tha**t life is all about fulfilling your potential and making the most of your precious time here on earth**. So, how do we go about cultivating this truly meaningful and enriching kind of existence?

To live a truly fulfilling life, there are certain 'needs' that we need to fulfil (quite literally) as human beings.

Different psychologists have hypothesised about what these different needs might be, and which ones are the most important. In the 1940s, for example, Abraham Maslow devised his famous **'hierarchy of needs'.** Maslow saw this hierarchy as structured like a pyramid, presenting a five-tier model for the needs that human beings need to 'tick off' in order to feel truly motivated and fulfilled in life.

Most ADVANCED	Self-Actualisation (desire to become the most that one can be; fulfilling your potential)
	Self-Esteem (respect, self-esteem, status, recognition, strength, freedom)
	Love and Belonging (friendship, intimacy, family, sense of connection)
	Safety (personal security, employment, resources, health, property)
Most BASIC (must be met first)	Physiological (Air, water, food, shelter, sleep clothing, reproduction)

The most basic of needs are, according to Maslow, our physiological and safety needs. They are the 'building blocks' for living a fulfilling life – without them, we could not survive, never mind thrive! They include those very basic needs of air, water, food, shelter, and sleep. They also include our need for personal security, good health, and access to basic resources.

Maslow believed that once these most basic of needs had been fulfilled, we could move up the hierarchy and find even greater life satisfaction through the attainment of love and belonging. **This included the formation of genuine friendships and relationships.** We are social animals with a deep need for love and connection – **without these strong and intimate relationships, it is impossible to feel fulfilled in life.**

After fulfiling our need for 'love and belonging', we can climb up the pyramid and strive to start fulfilling our need for 'self-esteem'. This reflects the human need for validation and some kind of status in life. **We all need to feel like what we are doing has value and that our work is being recognised – by both ourselves and also by other people.** We need **a strong sense of self-esteem in order to be motivated and fulfilled,** which effectively strengthens our sense of purpose in life. We all want to feel like we are making a difference and achieving something in this world – we are making our mark and leaving a legacy.

Believing you are someone worthy of praise, respect and recognition is an absolutely essential in order to feel like you are fulfilling your potential as a human being. I strongly believe that it **is nice to be liked, it is even better to be loved - but it is** *essential* **that you feel respected.**

Once we have ticked off all four of the lower tiers on the hierarchy - physiological, safety, love and belonging & self esteem - we can finally achieve what Maslow describes as 'self-actualisation'. This is what the Ancient Greek philosopher Aristotle - our main man - termed 'eudaimonia'. As we know, **eudaimonia means 'becoming the most that one can be' and fulfilling your potential as a human being.**

Let me remind you: **Nothing brings us greater happiness than fulfilling our potential and becoming the best version of ourselves.** This might be in our career or in our relationships – whatever area of life we are talking about, we want to feel that we are being the best version of ourselves and that we are making the best contribution that we possibly can.

When you achieve self-actualisation - which means fulfilling your potential - you can confidently say that you are 'living your best life'. As a result, you can be guaranteed to feel genuinely happy and fulfilled. **And by 'happy', I mean the unshakeable feeling of absolute bliss and contentment that is achieved when you are actively fulfiling your potential and living your life with a real sense of purpose!**

Here's what I strongly believe: **If you want to become truly happy in your life, you need to start making fulfilment your new focus!** Forget about pursuing pleasure, wealth, attention or validation! Focus instead on finding genuine, meaningful and lost-lasting fulfilment! **At all times, be focused on the goal of self-actualisation and becoming the best version of yourself.**

Work your way up Maslow's five-tier pyramid and you'll find that you're well on the way to flourishing through life!

Strive to firstly achieve your most basic needs and - at all times - keep your eyes fixed on that ultimate goal of self-actualisation. *Strive to make fulfilment your focus, and you will flourish through life!*

21. STOP MAKING EXCUSES

"It is possible to curb your arrogance, to overcome pleasure and pain, to rise above your ambition, and to not be angry with stupid and ungrateful people – yes, even to care for them" (Marcus Aurelius)

It is completely within your capabilities to transform your entire existence and become the very best version of yourself. Every resource that you need lies within your own very being... all that you need now is hard work and discipline.

This is the inspiring message at the heart of Stoicism, a philosophy for life first developed over 2,000 years ago. **The Stoics believed very strongly in the idea that we must all take full responsibility for our own lives. It is in fact your duty to become the master of your own destiny and the author of your own life.**

We can all live what the Stoics referred to as 'the good life' by cultivating **self-mastery, self-discipline, perseverance and wisdom.**

Stoic philosophy is built on the foundation of these so-called three 'disciplines' - the disciplines of perception, action and the will. According to the Stoics, we each have a duty to strengthen ourselves in these three disciplines in order to live good, resilient and fulfiling lives.

There is never any excuse for not cultivating the disciplines of perception, action and will in your life. Indeed, **stoicism refuses to accept any excuses <u>whatsoever!</u>** Under no circumstances did the Stoics believe you were allowed to outsource blame, responsibility or accountability for any area of your life. **It is instead 100% down to you to take accountability for your life, work hard to overcome your flaws, and to commit to living your very best life.**

In order to live your best life, you need to get more Stoical! You need to get serious about cultivating discipline of perception, action and will. This means that you need to stop hiding from reality and stop avoiding difficult truths! You need to stop spending your whole life hiding away in your comfort zones! **You need to take full responsibility for your entire life - If you want to live your best possible life, then you had better get out there and start creating it!**

There are no excuses for not making positive changes that will improve the quality of your life. This change must always come from within us – we must take responsibility for our happiness and success in life! That means **working tirelessly hard every single day to become the very best versions of ourselves. That means relentlessly facing our fears, boldly challenging our insecurities and consciously living purpose-driven lives!**

Here's what the Stoics believed: **life is tough, but you are tougher.** You need to realise that whilst life will throw all sorts of challenges at you, **you are more than capable of handling every single one of them**. You do not have to be a victim of life. You do not have to spend your days feeling sorry for yourself about what has happened to you!

One way of shaking off the victim mindset and taking back control of your life is **realising the difference between the things which you can control and things which you can't.**

The Stoics lived their lives by a concept called **'amor fati'**, which means to accept your fate. The idea is that we need to **stop complaining about things we cannot control or change and focus instead on the things that we can.** The Stoics believed we have to just accept the fact that life isn't always fair, and we must therefore strive to make peace with the fact that things will not always go our way.

There is absolutely no point struggling against the existence of suffering when it is just a fact of human existence!

Instead of wasting your energy denying the existence of adversity, you should channel your resources into confidently responding to it!

And if there is something that you simply cannot change or do anything about, then you must make it your mission to **stoically accept it and bravely carry your burden.**

The only thing that we ever have complete control over is our own thoughts. We therefore ought to focus all of our effort and energy on disciplining our mind, rather than trying to control the whole world.

This means that **we need to get serious about taking full responsibility for our thoughts, behaviours and beliefs.**

Success in life is not going to be handed to you on a plate - **to get what you want in life, you have to do all of the hard work yourself! You need to be disciplined about maintaining a 'mindset for success'!**

And the hard work to achieve that success starts right here and right now! There are therefore no excuses for not working hard to create a good life for both yourself and your family. **At**

the end of the day, it all comes down to YOU!

Stop putting off your personal transformation. Stop blaming other people or external circumstances for your lack of happiness or success. **Stop making excuses and avoiding taking accountability for your life!** At the end of the day, **it all comes down to you.**

So stop making those excuses and start making big changes. *The power to transform your life is entirely within your own hands.*

That is not to say that this transformation will be easy, but life is not about doing what is easy. There will be tears, tantrums and days when you feel like you can't do it.

There will be times when will feel exhausted, drained and utterly fed up. But feeling fed up is not an excuse to not keep getting up, putting yourself out there and working hard at turning all of your dreams into your brand new reality!

As Confucius once famously taught, **'our greatest glory is not in never falling, but in rising every time that we fall'.**

In order to live your best possible life, you need to commit yourself to working harder today than you have ever worked before.

Keep disciplined, keep persevering, and keep *growing* through everything that go through. Stop making excuses, start bravely carry your burdens...and start living more stoically!

22. MAKE INNER PEACE YOUR PRIORITY

"We can never obtain peace in the outer world until we make peace with ourselves" (Buddha)

Inner peace is the most important thing we can ever achieve as human beings.

The good news is this: **you can attain inner peace right here and right now...in this very present moment!**

So many people go through life desperately trying to find fulfilment and contentment. They think that they'll find it once they're finally in a relationship, or that they'll find it when they finally have more money than anybody else.

What they don't realise is that **the only place you can find genuine fulfilment and contentment is within yourself.** As the Buddha once said, **"Peace comes from within. Do not seek it without".**

In her bestselling book 'Eat, Pray, Love', Elizabeth Gilbert writes this: **"We don't realise that somewhere within us all, there does exist a supreme self who is eternally at peace".**

These words could not be more true! Although we may not realise it right now, each and every one of us has the most extraordinary capacity to experience genuine inner peace within themselves. **In a world of constant change, chaos and conflict, we can find true peace in this very present moment.**

I was first introduced to the concept of 'inner peace' by my therapist Sarah, who I was seeing as part of my recovery from the eating disorder anorexia. Sarah had spent a session talking to me about 'mindfulness', and when I got home that evening, I wanted to do some more research on this concept. I found myself reading articles about the practice of meditation and wanted to give it a go. I was already keenly interested in the study of religion, and had heard before about the Eastern origins of this spiritual discipline. I was intrigued to see that this ancient Buddhist practice was now being used as a 21st century psychotherapeutic tool.

And so that evening, I sat down in my bedroom and did my first ever session of meditation. And let me tell you with no exaggeration whatsoever here - that evening changed my life! More specifically, deciding to start practicing meditation changed my life!

When I talk to people about meditation, they often tell me that they're unsure about how it all works. They can't understand why you would just sit there with your legs crossed and make a conscious effort not to think about anything. *'Isn't that just a waste of time? some people will ask'*, or they might say, *'No, I couldn't do it because I can't stop myself from thinking even for 5 seconds!'*

I think a lot of people assume that meditation is going to be a lot harder than it looks. They imagine that you have to start chanting or even start levitating in the air! I can honestly tell you that meditation is the easiest practice in the world. **All that it requires is an open mind and a willingness to just sit with your breath for a short amount of time.**

When I first started meditation, I would meditate for around 15/20 minutes at a time. I would put on some relaxing background music - I always enjoyed putting on some Classic FM, or one of those sleep soundtracks that you find on YouTube! - and then I would simply sit on the end of my bed.

For those 15/20 minutes, I would allow myself to be fully present in the moment and become fully conscious of my breath. I found that my meditation sessions became sacred - I would look forward to having those 20 minutes of calm at the end of each day!

As time went on, I found myself really cherishing these sessions and wanting to meditate more and more. Meditation seemed to have the most extraordinary effect on me - after meditation, I was no longer worrying about what people were thinking about me or feeling so anxious about my appearance and identity. Instead, I found that I was becoming so much calmer and feeling so much more 'at peace' with myself. Meditation was making me feel so much more comfortable and content in my own skin - it was a truly extraordinary process!

So I decided that as well as meditating for 20 minutes every evening, I would make meditation part of my morning routine as well. I began setting my alarm for 6:30am every single morning, and began starting every single day with 30 minutes of meditation. I am not exaggerating when I say that this was the best decision that I have ever made!

I cannot begin to imagine what my life would be like today if I didn't start every single morning with my 30 minutes of meditation! This daily practice has completely and utterly transformed my entire life. My morning meditation sessions enable me to start every day - no matter where I am or what I am doing - with nothing but focus and inner peace. After my 30 minutes of meditation, I am 100% ready to take on the day!

It grounds me, calms me, and prepares me for the busy day ahead!

Meditation has become an absolute anchor in my busy life. My daily practice - and consistency is so important when it comes to practicing meditation - has enabled me to cultivate the most extraordinary sense of inner peace. Meditation has also supplied me with the most incredible self-awareness, self-confidence and self-discipline. I passionately believe that it is the most positive and transformative practice any of us can ever choose to begin in our lives. *What's more, meditation is completely free and can be practiced anywhere and at anytime!*

When people ask me how I was able to overcome my eating disorder and turn my life around, I honestly tell them that the practice of meditation was my secret weapon! By starting every morning with my 30 minutes of mindful reflection, I have been able to cultivate the most extraordinary level of self-awareness and self-confidence. To this day, **meditation continues to provide me with the most incredible sense of inner strength, self-awareness and inner peace**.

As you can tell by now, I have become the world's biggest advocate for the practice of meditation! It is such a simple yet transformative practice, and I passionately believe that it should be taught in every single school across the world. As His Holiness the Dalai Lama says, **'if every 8 year old in the world is taught meditation, we would eliminate violence from the world within one generation'.** I'd add to this that if everybody in the Western world took up the practice of meditation, we would also eliminate so much of the anxiety, depression and unhappiness that so millions of people are suffering from.

But whilst meditation is an excellent way of cultivating inner peace in your life, it is certainly not the *__only__* way! So if meditation isn't necessarily your cup of (green) tea, then don't worry! **Because there are <u>many</u> paths to a life of inner peace!**

The most important thing you should know about inner peace is that **<u>it is a choice</u>**. It is a choice to realise that whatever happens in your life, you can handle it. It is a choice to realise that your worth is not dependent on external factors but on the unconditional value of your human life. **It is a choice to look for calm, contentment and fulfilment within your own very soul.**

Here's what you need to know: **There is no reason why you cannot achieve genuine inner peace right here and right now in this very present moment.** You do not need to be a Buddhist monk meditating in the Himalayas in order to find inner peace – you can achieve inner peace no matter how busy your life is or how much conflict and chaos is going on in the world around you!

With that in mind, I want to share with you 8 ways you can cultivate inner peace in this very moment:

- **Accept Yourself Unconditionally.** You must fully accept and embrace yourself as you are. You must commit yourself to living a truly authentic life. You, just as much as anybody else in the whole entire universe, deserve to live a happy and fulfilling life. Happiness begins with honesty and authenticity – you need to be completely comfortable in your own skin. You need to detach from conditions of worth, absolutist thinking, and the pressures of perfectionism. You are enough as you are – you are whole and you have intrinsic worth as a conscious human being. In order to have inner peace, you must have unconditional self-acceptance. You have nothing to prove and nothing to fear – give yourself the love you deserve.

- **Stop Struggling Against The Universe**. Stop getting angry about things over which you have no control. Stop thinking that you are a victim of the universe and start believing that you are the master of your own destiny. Know that whatever happens in life, you can handle it. Try not to see the universe as a force acting against you – remember that 'life is not a problem to be solved but a reality to be experienced' (Kierkegaard). Every single person faces suffering in their life – we cannot eliminate pain, and we shouldn't even attempt to. The cessation of suffering is not achieved by extinguishing it altogether but by rising above it. We must accept that life is filled with suffering, struggle and setbacks – this is nothing personal but part of the way the world works. Sickness and death come to us all – they are simply facts of life. Remember that **people are 'not disturbed by things, but by the view they take of them' (Epictetus).** Stop labelling everything as 'good' or 'bad' and learn to enjoy living life as a journey. We can learn from every setback we face and see each challenge as an opportunity for growth. No matter what happens in your life, you can handle it. External events and situations cannot take away the inner peace within you.

- Meditate every morning. Start everyday with 20-30 minutes of silent meditation. Set an alarm for the same time every single morning and be disciplined in sticking to it. For the duration of your meditation, focus on your breathing and simply observing your thoughts. Let those thoughts, feelings, impulses and ideas come and go. Acknowledge that they are there, observe them for a moment, and then let them go on their way. Recognise that you are not your thoughts and that you do not have to be driven by your impulses. Focus on cultivating a sense of calm within you and a feeling of connection with the present moment. Spend this time simply appreciating the fact that you are alive. When you find yourself distracted, repeat this mantra to yourself: 'I am deeply thankful to be here in this present moment'. Make meditation part of your daily routine and watch how life becomes so much more fulfilling.

- Be fully present in this moment. As Eckhart Tolle reminds us, we must **'realise deeply that the present moment is all you ever have'**. If you are not present in this very moment, you cannot expect to find inner peace within yourself. We must anchor ourselves in the breath and fully 'show up' to each situation life presents us with. Distractions such as social media scrolling stop us from fully connecting with where we are now. Allow yourself to be awake and attentive in this very moment – it is all you will ever have! Be deeply thankful for this present moment and strive to completely connect with exactly where you are in life right now.

- Put everything into perspective. Whenever you feel yourself getting caught up in a situation, make a conscious effort to look at the scenario from a wider perspective. Step outside of yourself in that moment and imagine you are looking down on the situation from another planet. How significant is this situation in the grand scheme of things? In this vast, ever-expanding universe does this problem really matter? In the grand scheme of your whole entire life, is this situation really such a big deal? Is the world going to stop turning because of what is going on in your life right this second? Remember that whatever is happening, you can handle it. Remember that this situation is microscopic when viewed from outer space – see the bigger picture and stop the situation from having an unnecessary amount of power over you. You will survive and the world will keep on turning.

- Know that whatever happens, you can handle it. This links very closely to putting everything into perspective. To have inner peace you need to realise that your worth as a human being is not dependent on external successes or other people's approval. Remember, you have unconditional value and worth as a human being. No matter what is happening in the world around you, remain confident in your own self and remain aware of your own worth. Whatever happens in the world around you, there is no reason to worry – you can handle it. There is a way through this situation, there is always a light at the end of the tunnel. We grow through everything that we go through – you have within you the strength to survive whatever challenge you are faced with. Remembering this will prevent you from being overwhelmed by the pressures of external challenges you might face as you go through life.

- Live with integrity. You cannot find inner peace if you do not have integrity as a human being. Deceit, insincerity and causing harm to others causes nothing but harm to ourselves. If you are not living in accordance with your values and with a spirit of sincerity, you will never find contentment within yourself. You must be truly accountable for your actions and feel that you have a 'clear conscience' in order to feel genuinely at peace. At all times, strive to conduct yourself with integrity – be true to yourself and treat other people with respect. Imagine that God was holding you to account on the Day of Judgement: would you be able to look your creator in the eye and say you were proud of the way you had conducted yourself? If you do not feel this sense of pride, it will be impossible to find inner peace. Integrity is everything.

- Strive to be the best version of yourself. In every situation, hold your head up high and strive to be the best version of yourself. Fulfil your potential and do the best that you can. We achieve true contentment when our 'ideal self' aligns with our 'actual self' – Carl Rogers described this achieving a state of 'congruence'. Whatever it is you are doing, strive to achieve this state of congruence – give it your all and make the best contribution that you can. Inner peace is achieved when we connect with our purpose, which is to strive to be the best version of ourselves in each situation.

In summary, cultivating **Inner peace is absolutely essential in order to live a happy and fulfilling life.** It is your most important anchor and your most important source of contentment in this world. You will never be able to thrive as a human being unless you start cultivating inner peace in this very moment that you have right now! **So stop searching for fulfilment and contentment through external experiences and instead allow yourself to find peace from within!**

Try a bit of meditation and try to live the whole of your life a little bit more mindfully - **make inner peace your new daily priority!** The most important thing to remember is that **inner peace is accessible to all of us in every single moment of our lives.** Indeed, it is accessible to us with every single breath that we take.

Your very current situation provides you with an extraordinary opportunity to become peace. So may you seize this opportunity to anchor yourself in inner peace. *Because the present moment is the only thing that we will ever have...*

23. MAKE CONENCTION YOUR CURRENCY

"Before you have finished breakfast in the morning you have already depended on more than half of the world" (Martin Luther King)

A happy and fulfilling life is one that is filled with genuine relationships and meaningful connections. Human beings are social animals who cannot survive+ without support and co-operation from others. From the moment that we are born until the moment that we die, we are completely dependent on other people in order to survive.

In our first few years of life, for example, we depend entirely on our parents and primary caregivers. The only thing a baby can do on its own is breathe! Without the love and care of other human beings, we wouldn't last more than a couple of hours. We depend on our parents for absolutely everything – our survival through the first few years of life is entirely depended on the formation of a strong connection between caregiver and child.

From the very first days of our human lives, it could not be clearer - the formation of strong and meaningful relationships is essential for our survival. Without these essential relationships and connections, we would not be here today. No man is an island, and no baby is able to bring themselves up!

And this dependency on other people does not suddenly disappear the moment that we are able to dress ourselves! **Throughout our whole lives, we remain dependent on the support and co-operation of other people in order to succeed as human beings.** For everything from the food we eat to the public transport systems we travel on, we depend on the hard work of other people.

Dr Martin Luther King put it perfectly in his famous Christmas Eve Sermon of 1967:

"It really all boils down to this: that all life is interrelated. We are all caught in an inescapable network of mutuality, tied into a single garment of destiny. Whatever affects one directly, affects all indirectly. We are made to live together because of the interrelated structure of reality. Did you ever stop to think that you can't leave for your job in the morning without being dependent upon most of the world? You get up in the morning and go to the bathroom and reach over for the sponge, and that's handed to you by a Pacific Islander. You reach for a bar of soap, and that's given to you at the hands of a Frenchman. And then you go into the kitchen to drink your coffee for the morning and that is poured into your cup by a South American. And maybe you want your tea: that's poured into your cup by a Chinese. Or maybe you have a desire for cocoa for breakfast, and that's poured into your cup by a West African. And then you reach over for your toast, and that's given you at the hands of an English speaking farmer, not to mention the baker. And before you've finished eating breakfast in the morning, you've depended on more than half the world".

Martin Luther King had a very powerful and important message to share with us here: **All life is interrelated.**

As human beings, we are not just dependent on our primary caregivers and immediate family and friends, but **are also dependent on the whole entire world**. We need to realise that we are all one humanity and that all life is interrelated and interdependent.

Across the globe, there are over 7 billion human beings.. and the truth is that every single one of them is just like us! Race, ethnicity, religion, sexual orientation and nationality are all completely irrelevant – at the end of the day, we are all just human beings. As St Paul wrote in his letter to the Galatians, **"there is neither Jew nor Greek, slave nor free, male nor female...for you are all one in Christ" (Galatians 3:28).**

How how does this belief that all life is interrelated transform the way in which we think and behave? How might the knowledge that we are all one humanity influence the way we approach the people we meet in our day-to-day lives? His Holiness the Dalai Lama puts it like this: **"Whenever I meet people I always approach them from the standpoint of the most basic things we have in common. We each have a physical structure, a mind, emotions. We are all born in the same way, and we all die. All of us want happiness and do not want to suffer".**

Holding this kind of outlook - where we see all of humanity as one and view all life as interrelated - has extraordinary benefits for us all.

As the Dalai Lama explains, **"Looking at others from this standpoint rather than emphasizing secondary differences** such as the fact I am a different colour, religion or cultural background, allows me to have a feel that I'm meeting someone just the same as me. I find that relating to others on that level makes it much easier to exchange and communicate with one another".

I strongly believe that when we meet people, we need to keep one primary goal in mind – **to connect with them . And the easiest way to achieve this is by focusing on the things that we have in common.**

Here's the thing: **We are all human beings and we all share that fundamental desire for happiness, love, acceptance and belonging.** *We are all inter-related and are we are all dependent on one another for everything from food and clothing to education and entertainment.*

Just think about it: how do you think the food on your plate managed to end up right here in front of you? How do you think the clothes you are wearing ended up in your wardrobe? **Every human being is interconnected, and we all belong to one universal human family.**

We need to realise that connection is the most powerful currency we possess. We should be looking for every opportunity to reach out to other human beings and form genuine relationships.

As William Butler Yeats once said, **'there are no strangers here; Only friends you haven't met yet'.** As you go into every social situation, anticipate that you will make friends, not enemies. Focus your mind on the things that you have in common with the people in the room, rather than dwelling on the surface-level and superficial factors that might divide you.

Each human being is – deep down – just the same as you. Each human being wants to be happy and loved in the same way as you do. When we keep this in mind, we realise that **we have a lot more in common with the rest of humanity than we originally thought!**

Here's what you need to know: **anything that brings you closer to other people is guaranteed to be good for your soul.** Any activity that builds bridges, forms relationships, and allows you to connect with other human beings is always a good thing. Seize every opportunity to get closer to other people and get to know them on a very human level.

Nothing is more important than forming meaningful connections and cultivating genuine relationships with our fellow human beings.

See beyond the superficial differences that separate different social groups and approach every single person as a human being.

Remember that we are all one humanity and are therefore all on this journey through life together!

If you want to to thrive through life, you need to start realising that connection is the most powerful currency you possess. You need to start making more meaningful connections and start approaching every single person you meet with a real attitude of openness.

Remember that **every single person has something to teach you and so make it your mission to learn from every conversation!** Remember to **focus on what you have in common** and **seize every opportunity to connect**. *This is what living a happy, meaningful and fulfilling life is all about!*

24. CULTIVATE MEANINGFUL RELATIONSHIPS

"Lots of people want to ride with you in the limo, but what you want is someone who will take the bus with you when the limo breaks down" (Oprah Winfrey)

One thing that will always guarantee you a meaningful life is the formation of meaningful relationships.

Friendships and relationships that are based on true feelings of affection bring our lives a real feeling of contentment and purpose.

In order to live a truly fulfilling life, you must commit yourself to the cultivation of genuinely fulfilling relationships.

I believe that contemporary social relationships fall into two broad categories: those that are 'transactional' and those that are based on genuine feelings of affection and connection.

Allow me to explain: A transactional relationship is one that is based on convenience or need – for example, a relationship with a potential investor, business client or casual sexual partner. You are using this relationship to get something – it is based on your needs and is more of a business transaction than a genuine relationship.

Transactional relationships are very effective at fulfiling many of the social needs that we all have in our busy lives. For example, if two people have a physical desire for sex and nothing more, then a consensual sexual arrangement can benefit them both.

As long as both people involved know that it is a purely physical and sexual 'transaction', then no one will get hurt or over-invest.

Similarly, there are a lot of benefits to forming so-called 'friendships of convenience'. These are friendships based on social status, shared workplace or any other surface-level factor. They can be mutually beneficial and help us out at certain times in our lives. Again, they are effective at fulfiling a temporary need in our busy lives.

However, it is important that you always enter this kind of transactional relationship with your eyes wide open. You need to know exactly what is going on, because there is nothing wrong with having 'transactional' relationships **as long as you are aware of exactly what your intentions are**.

In other words, don't get emotionally invested in a relationship that is nothing more than a business deal or a 'hook up' for sex!

Don't believe that you have a genuine and meaningful friendship with someone when in reality they are just friends with you because of your social status or bank balance!

I like to think of it like this: it is nice to be seen as attractive, it is even better to be seen as dateable or even loveable - but it is *essential to be respected.* Every single relationship that you have must be based on mutual appreciation and respect - in other words, don't let somebody use you, walk all over you and leave you looking like a complete fool!

It's important to realise that transactional relationships – where we are using other people in order to satisfy our needs - will only ever fulfil <u>temporary</u> needs. They might fulfil our need for sexual pleasure, for example, or help us to secure the business deal that we desperately need.

But if we want to have a genuinely happy and fulfilling life, I believe that transactional relationships are simply not enough. Whilst they might satisfy specific temporary needs in the short term, transactional relationships are never able to provide us with the genuine intimacy, connection, and unconditional love that we all need as human beings. That's because transactional relationships are never based on that all-important mutual appreciation and respect. They are instead driven by selfish impulses and desires, and will therefore never fulfil us as human beings!

When it comes to our friendships and relationships, we need something more meaningful than just the fulfilment of a need. You deserve to be respected, appreciated and treated properly! The 'meaningful' kind of relationship is the kind based on what the Buddhist spiritual leader His Holiness the Dalai Lama describes as 'true human feeling'.

Here's what he writes:

"Some friendships are based on wealth, power, or position. In these cases, your friendship continues as long as your power, wealth or position is sustained. Once these grounds are no longer there, then the friendship will also begin to disappear. On the other hand, there is another kind of friendship. Friendships that are based not on considerations of wealth,

power and position but rather on true human feeling, a feeling of closeness in which there is a sense of sharing and connectedness".

This kind of meaningful relationship is sustained by "a feeling of affection", which obviously very different to a relationship that is being driven by feelings of lust or a desire for status and power.

Only this kind of meaningful relationship is truly fulfilling and sustainable, which it is why it is so important to be actively cultivating this type of relationship throughout your life.

Get serious about forming meaningful genuine connections with the people that you meet as you go through life. *Seek something meaningful as opposed to seeing life as one big business transaction!* People are not products to be disposed of when they no longer fulfil our needs or serve a transactional purpose!

If you take the 'transactional' approach to relationships, then prepare yourself for a lifetime lacking any sense of fulfilment or purpose! **We must seize every opportunity to connect with other human beings in a sincere and meaningful way.**

Research has shown that we become like the average of the five people we spend the most time with. Hal Elrod writes that **'who you spend your time with may become the single most determining factor in the person you become and in your quality of life'**. It is therefore essential that you surround yourself with authentic, genuine and honest people. As Elrod writes: "**Spend time with positive, successful achievers and inevitably their attitudes and successful habits will reflect**

on you. You'll become more and more like them". Conversely, if you spend all of your time with fake, selfish and untrustworthy people, then your life will become a very insecure, shallow and miserable place indeed!

I don't know about you, but nothing fills me with more happiness than spending time with the people I love. These are the people who you know unconditionally love, support and respect you. In my life, my family and best friends are everything. It is these deeply meaningful relationships that give my life meaning and purpose - I could not achieve anything or do anything in my life without the unconditional love and support of my family and closest friends.

It is within the framework of these meaningful relationships that we can truly dare to be vulnerable.

As Brene Brown writes: **"Vulnerability is based on mutuality and requires boundaries and trust. It's not oversharing... it's not indiscriminate disclosure, and it's not celebrity-style social media information dumps. Vulnerability is about sharing our feelings and our experiences with people who have earned the right to hear them. Being vulnerable and open is mutual and an integral part of the trust-building process"**.

I strongly believe that it is only when we anchor our relationships in these genuine feelings of openness, affection, and care that we can start living truly fulfilling and enriching lives.

Relationships should never be based on someone's wealth, social status, physical attractiveness, or what they can 'do' for you.

A relationship is not about using someone as a means to an end. A relationship is instead about thinking about someone with a genuine 'feeling of affection'.

As the Dalai Lama says: **"If one is seeking to build a truly sat-**

isfying relationship, the best way of bringing this about is to get to know the deeper nature of the person and relate to them on that level, instead of merely relying on superficial characteristics".

I therefore believe that you must **make the formation of meaningful relationships and genuine connections your absolute priority**! Strive to move beyond the superficial interests of appearance, money and social status.

Aspire instead to develop relationships that are grounded in a sense of genuine connection and unshakeable commitment!

In her book 'The Gifts of Imperfection', Brene Brown shares this definition of love:

"We cultivate love when we allow our most vulnerable and powerful selves to be deeply seen and known, and when we honour the spiritual connection that grows from offering with trust, respect, kindness and affection. Love is not something we give or get; it is something that we need nurture and grow, a connection that can only be cultivated between two people when it exists within each one of them - we can only love others as much as we love ourselves".

It is absolutely clear that this genuine and meaningful kind of **'love' can only ever be fully expressed within the framework of a genuinely meaningful relationship.** It cannot be exchanged in a transactional or business-like manner but must instead be fully actualised within an authentic relationship grounded in mutual affection and trust. I strongly believe this: **the more meaningful relationships that you can cultivate in your life, the better!** They bring so much fulfilment, happiness and give your life a whole new sense of purpose.

Anna Taylor said something important about this kind of genuinely meaningful friendship: **"Some people arrive and make such a beautiful impact on your life, you can barely remember what life was like without them"**.

This is what friendships and relationships should be all about – connection, commitment, and the desire to genuinely make a difference in someone's life.

To do this, **we have to approach people with a spirit of affection and compassion.** We have to aspire to achieve authentic intimacy and genuine connection in our relationships with others.

If you want to enjoy a meaningful life, then **make it your mission to form as many meaningful connections and relationships as possible.** Use transactional relationships if you must, but remember that they can never truly fulfil you or enrich your life.

Get out there and start forging genuinely authentic and affectionate friendships! Dare to be deeply loving and vulnerable in your relationships!

As Aristotle once wrote, **'friendship is a single soul dwelling in two bodies'**.

Stop caring about transactional friendships of convenience and get serious about cultivating high-quality connections with other human beings!

Make your life truly meaningful by filling it with as genuine and meaningful relationships as you can!

25. MOVE BEYOND FEAR

"Whatever happens, you can handle it" (Susan Jeffers)

In order to live our lives to the full, we need to learn how to move beyond our fears.

We need to stop letting worry and anxiety rule over our lives, and start living by this life-changing mantra instead: **Whatever happens, you can handle it.**

The feeling of fear has the power to paralyse us in a way that nothing else in the entire universe can. For many people, life is driven not by the pursuit of fulfilment but by feelings of fear. The worst thing is that most people don't even know what it is they are scared or anxious about – they simply have a fear of fear.

To take back control of our lives, we need to make friends with fear. We need to realise that fear is only able to limit our lives and control our minds if we let it.

According to 'The Fear Bubble', a brilliant book written by the S.A.S Special Forces sniper Ant Middleton, there are three primary types of fear: the fears of suffering, failure, and conflict. Underpinning these three types of fear is one ultimate fear - the fear of not being good enough. That's right - **The fear of not being good enough is everyone's secret fear.**

I strongly believe that if we can overcome this fear of not **being good enough, then we can solve all of our problems.** It sounds very simple and straightforward, doesn't it! So how do we actually go about overcoming this fear of not being good enough? How do we actively move beyond fear? **The goal is to replace your fear of not being good enough with a commitment to a life of self-growth.**

As JK Rowling once said, **"It is impossible to live without failing at something...unless you live so cautiously that you might as well not have lived at all - in which case, you fail by default".** We need to replace our fear of failure with a confident belief that *whatever happens in life, I can handle it!*

Seriously, what is the worst that can actually happen? Can the 'worst case' outcome really be worse than living your entire life as a hostage to your fears?

Are you really going to let your fear of 'not being good enough' stop you from doing the things that you love and becoming the best version of yourself?

Instead of being overwhelmed by your fears, you need to keep focused on fulfilling your purpose in life. Recognise that fear is real...but then also **recognise that fear can only have power over your life if you let it!** In order to take back control of your life, you need to get confident at acknowledging your feeling of fear before choosing to move beyond it.

I strongly believe that **the only reason fear exists is to be conquered!** And in order to conquer your fears, here's what you need to know: **your worth is not dependent on the number of successes and the number of failures you have had in your life.** If things go wrong, which from time-to-time they inevitably will, **you will survive!**

It's time we started to realise that **Fear is not your enemy but** can in fact actually become your friend!Making friends with fear begins with realising that whatever happens in your life, you can handle it!

That is not to say that you should never *feel* fear – fear is, of course, a very natural human emotion. Indeed, it serves us an essential early warning signal that tells us when there is a potential risk of harm. *But the moment fear is able to start paralysing us is the moment you need to realise it is no longer serving any positive purpose in your life!*

In order to live a genuinely fulfilling life, **you need to start harnessing that feeling of fear and refuse to let it paralyse you.** In other words, you need to start feeling the fear…and do the things that scare you most anyway!

Remember that fear is not the enemy! **Without fear there is no challenge and without challenge, there is no growth.** We need to be challenged and forced to confront our fears in order to grow as human beings. **We need to be tested and forced to step outside of our comfort zones, because this is when the *really* magic happens!**

So if you feel anxious about being served by someone in the supermarket, make it your mission that day to strike up a conversation with the person serving you.

If you feel anxious about walking past a certain group of people on your way to school, make it your mission to walk past them with your head held high. Don't let yourself get away with it by saying 'oh I'll do it tomorrow' or 'no I'm too scared'.

Face your fears head-on – you'll find that not only do you survive the experience, but that it wasn't half as bad as your thoughts had made it out to be!

We need to move beyond the fear that paralyses us and prevents us from becoming the best version of ourselves.

Make friends with fear –acknowledge that it is there and then move beyond it. Know that whatever happens, you can handle it. Know that you *need* to be challenged in order to grow and become the best version of yourself.

Most importantly, know that overcoming the paralysing effects of fear is as simple as saying 'f*ck you fear, I'm going to do it anyway!

Start daring to do more of the things that scare you, and dare to boldly move beyond your fears!

26. THE CULTIVATION OF CHARACTER

"The truly good and wise man will bear all kinds of fortune in a seemly way, and will always act in the noblest manner that the circumstances allow" (Aristotle)

We live in a society that is utterly obsessed with the idea that you can buy your way to happiness and fulfilment. Our society believes that the secret to being happy is getting as rich, famous, and beautiful as you possibly can be.

If you don't have the latest sports car, designer wardrobe, and a botox-injected forehead, then nobody is going to believe for a second that you could possibly be living your best life!

Well I hate to break it to our accumulation-obsessed society, but this approach to happiness is completely and utterly wrong. That's because **happiness is not something that can be be bought and sold.**

Whilst there is nothing wrong whatsoever with enjoying the finer things in life, **we need to realise that happiness cannot be achieved through the relentless pursuit of pleasure. Instead, genuine happiness and flourishing in life is achieved through the cultivation of strong moral character.**

The idea that happiness and flourishing can be achieved through the cultivation of character is found in both Eastern and Western philosophy. In the West, Aristotle first wrote about the importance of character over 2,500 years ago, when he devised his ethical theory known today as 'Virtue Ethics'.

Aristotle believed that if we wanted to become truly happy human beings, **we must strive to become virtuous individuals who conduct ourselves with moral integrity at all times**. He believed very strongly that happiness is achieved through the cultivation of character and virtue, which enables us to enjoy what the Greeks famously termed 'the good life'.

Happiness, wrote Aristotle, is an "activity of the soul". He reveals in his famous 'Nicomachean Ethics' that **"even if happiness is not sent [to] us from heaven, but is won by virtue and by some kind of study or practice, it seems to be one of the most divine things that exist".**

There we have it - **happiness is 'won by virtue'.** It could not be clearer - in order to live a happy and fulfiling life, we must **practice virtue and commit to the cultivation of a strong moral character!**

Aristotle believed that **"the life of active virtue is essentially pleasant"**, and that true happiness was achieved by a commitment to the cultivation of a virtuous character. **This means that you must dedicate your life to the development of both moral and intellectual virtues in your life.**

You need to commit yourself to a life of integrity, through the development of strong moral virtues that will anchor and define you as a human being. Aristotle suggested an extensive number of virtues that he believed human beings ought to cultivate in order to live a happy and fulfilling life. These included **bravery, modesty, temperance, justice, liberality, sincerity, endurance, wisdom, and dignity.**

For Aristotle, it wasn't enough to just believe in the importance of these virtues - **he believed very strongly that you needed to put them into practice in your everyday life!** He believed that **human beings "are what we repeatedly do",** arguing that 'excellence is not an act but a habit'. **We therefore have to practice what we preach and put our virtues into practice on every single day of our lives!**

It wasn't just the Ancient Greeks who believed that the cultivation of virtue was the secret to living a happy and fulfilling life. In the Christian tradition, for example, there is a commitment to the development of personal integrity and moral character. St Paul writes to the Colossians that they should **"clothe yourselves with compassion, kindness, humility, gentleness, and patience".**

The Stoic philosophers were also very passionate about the art of virtuous living, with Epictetus writing in one letter; **"The good are virtues and all that share in them; the bad are the vices and all that indulge in them".**

In Eastern philosophy, there is a remarkably similar focus on the importance of cultivating character. At the very heart of Buddhism we find the concept of the 'Eightfold Path'. This is an ancient teaching grounded in the idea that in order to attain liberation from earthly suffering, we must cultivate right action, right thought and right understanding.

The eightfold path consists of the following 8 practices:

- **Right View**
- **Right Mindfulness**
- **Right Concentration**

- **Right Effort**

- **Right Livelihood**

- **Right Action**

- **Right Speech**

- **Right Intention**

By following this eightfold path, Buddhists believe that they can cultivate strong moral character and so attain liberation from their earthly suffering. The virtues serve as a powerful antidote to the so-called 'three poisons' of greed, hatred and ignorance.

In the Mahayanan tradition of Buddhism, there are a further 'six perfections' that Buddhists are encouraged to cultivate. They are:

- **Generosity**

- **Morality**

- **Patience**

- **Energy**

- **Meditation**

- **Wisdom**

The Buddhist practitioner strives to cultivate these perfections within themselves - it is all about the development of their moral character as a human being.

In both the eastern and western imagination, living 'the good life' all comes down to the cultivation of moral character through the practice of strong moral virtues. In both Christianity and Buddhism, it is not enough to simply 'do' good when you feel like it or when other people are watching. At all times, you have an obligation to embody strong moral virtues and to become a person who proudly possesses strong moral character . It is your divinely-appointed responsibility to conduct yourself with absolute moral integrity.

Happiness is not the product of endlessly pursuing pleasure, but is instead the result of living a genuinely virtuous life. **This means fulfiling your potential as a human being through the cultivation of a strong moral character.**

You need to be committed to the cultivation of strong moral virtues and committed to living a life of complete accountability and integrity.

In order to achieve this, you need to know exactly what virtues you believe in and - most importantly - actively put them into practice every single day of your life!

Live a genuinely meaningful and fulfilling life by making it your mission to cultivate strong moral character!

27. KNOW THAT CHANGE IS THE ONLY CONSTANT IN LIFE

"To improve is to change; to be perfect is to change often" (Winston Churchill)

The vast majority of us – myself included - are real creatures of comfort.

We deeply cherish our daily routines and the reliable rhythms of human life. As human beings, we really do love any kind of routine and regularity in our lives. We take it for granted that the sun will rise every morning and that that every 25 December we will sit around the dinner table with our family and enjoy a delicious Christmas dinner. We take it for granted when we go to bed in the evening that when we wake up the world will be exactly the same as it was the night before.

We ALL take comfort in familiarity and we all get complacent about life's little customs. It's a very human thing to do! As the 18th century philosopher David Hume famously once said, **'custom is the great guide of life'.** We like the fact that our diaries are filled with reliable fixtures, such as Christmas and the summer holidays.

We like the fact that we take the same commute to the office every single morning and love the fact that when we return home that evening we'll be able to watch our favourite shows on at their usual times in the schedule. There is something very reassuring about certainty – it gives us a feeling of comfort and the belief that we have some amount of control in this often unsettling and uncertain world.

Whilst there is nothing at all wrong with finding comfort in your daily routines and annual rituals, *we must be sure not to let our love for comfort make us resistant to change.*

It is a fact of human existence that change is the only constant in life. As the Stoic Philosopher Marcus Aurelius wrote in his diaries over 2,000 years ago, **"All things are in a process of change. You yourself are subject to constant alteration and gradual decay. So too is the whole universe".**

Change is just a fact of life. It is what drives the universe and keeps everything in motion. Without change, there would be no life. **Without change, there would no future for any of us! Absolutely everything is subject to change….and this is absolutely nothing to be scared of!**

According to the Buddhist religion, it is the eternal truth of the universe that not a single thing is permanent. Even human beings are subject to constant change! *Just think about it - are you the same person today as you were on the day that you were born?* Scientists tell us that the human body replaces itself with a completely new set of cells every 7-10 years. The idea of a fixed and stable 'self' is nothing more than a Western illusion! That's right, **even YOU are in a constant state of transformation and change!**

As a result, it is totally unhealthy to keep struggling against the process of change. It is absolutely ludicrous to keep clinging onto the comfort offered to us by adherence to customs.

There is absolutely nothing we can do to stop change from happening; **change is going to happen every single day of our lives whether we like it or not!**

No matter how desperately you want all things to forever remain the same, **the circle of life will always keep turning and the seasons of the year will always keep changing.**

Everything in the entire universe is constantly subjected to transformation and change - it is impossible to make time stand still!

And so it is clear to me that we have a very choice: **we can continue struggling against change, or we can choose to bravely accept it instead.** I wonder if you can guess which one of these two choices I will be advocating?!

In order to live a happy and fulfilling life, we need to accept the fact that change is the only constant in life. If there is only one thing that you can be certain of in this universe, it is that **nothing will ever stay the same. Fighting against this will get you absolutely nowhere. You need to embrace the existence of change and make a conscious decision to enjoy the journey.**

Confidently take on every new challenge that comes your way and **at all times strive to keep moving forwards in your life! Strive to be someone who accepts change and stoically embraces every opportunity it provides you with!**

Now, I do realise that making peace with the inescapability of change is a lot easier said than done. So how should we go about dealing with change?

What mindset should we maintain when it comes to understanding the ever-changing nature of our universe?

There's a mantra that I use every single morning to remind myself of the fact that change is the only constant in life.

It is this: 'Let it come, let it be, let it go'. 'Let it come, let it be, let it go'. *Instead of struggling against change, we need to develop a much greater tolerance for it.*

We need to make peace with the fact that nothing is ever permanent and that we need to constantly keep moving forwards.

It is, of course, perfectly healthy to retain strong connections to people and places from your past. But we must realise that it is impossible to turn back the clock or even just pause time for one second.

As autonomous human beings, we have to continuously keep choosing to embrace change and fully accept that it is the only constant in our lives. Here's the important thing that you need to know: <u>**just because things change, this does not mean you have no control over your life.**</u>

As autonomous and rational human beings, we do in fact have a lot of control over **the direction of the change that in our lives.** Indeed, I passionately believe that **life is 10% what happens to you and 90% how you choose to respond.**

Change is inevitable, but it always comes with a choice. You always have the *choice* to use change as a positive catalyst for personal growth and self development in your life. As the British Wartime Prime Minister Winston Churchill once said,: **"There is nothing wrong with change…if it is in the right direction".** And so you must be continuously choosing to embrace change as a positive opportunity to grow as a human being.

Every single time that we embrace change in our lives, we become even more fearless and empowered individuals. When we make peace with the fact that change is the only constant in life - and start seeing change as a very positive opportunity for growth - we finally **stop struggling against the universe and start to enjoy our journey through life.**

Instead, here's what I believe: **Stop struggling against the process and allow yourself to thrive through it instead.** It's time to master the art of letting things go and commit yourself to learning through every challenge that you endure. Life, said the existentialist philosopher Kierkegaard, is not a problem to be solved but a reality to be experienced.

Accept the fact that change is the only constant in life. Realise that it is down to you whether change has a positive or negative impact on your life. **Stop struggling against the process and choose to thrive through it instead! Realise that you grow through everything that you go through!**

Get committed to learning through every single challenge that you face in your life. Get serious about appreciating every moment for what it is. Remember that whatever happens, you can handle it. Whatever happens, remember to **to let it come, let it be and let it go.**

Stop clinging on to comfort and start embracing the opportunities provided by change instead!

28. KNOW YOURSELF

"Knowing yourself is the beginning of all wisdom" (Aristotle)

How well do you actually know yourself? To what extent do you actually know who you are and what you stand for as a human being?

There is no greater task in life than knowing and accepting who you authentically are. In the words of the great philosopher Socrates, **'the unexamined life is not worth living'**.

If you want to live your best life and become the very best version of yourself, it goes without saying that you need to know who you are and get confident in your own skin! In order to be a success in life, it is essential that you have a serious amount of self-awareness.

What is it that makes you unique in this world? What are your biggest sources of happiness? What excites you and what scares you the most? If you had the freedom to live your life in whatever way you fancied – in a world where money or public opinion was of no issue whatsoever – how would you choose to live your life?

When you start to ask yourself these kinds of important questions, you are able to start working out exactly who you are and exactly what it means to be the best version of your-

self.

Here are just a couple of questions that I think you'd really benefit from asking yourself today - see how you get on...

- Who am I?
- What is the meaning of life?
- Am I true to myself every day?
- When am I at my best in life?
- What is my favourite way to spend a day?
- What am I most scared of in life?
- What are my biggest fears in life?
- What would my 'dream life' look like?
- What kind of person do I want to be in this world?
- What things do I value the most in my life?
- Who are the most important people in my life right now?
- How would I describe myself?
- How do I think other people would describe me?
- What defence mechanisms do I most frequently deploy?
- What is my definition of a successful life?
- What are three of my biggest strengths?
- What are three of my biggest weaknesses?
- If I knew this was my last day on earth, what would I do?
- Are you more of a talker or a listener?
- Do you feel happiest in small groups / alone or in larger social settings?
- What do you feel – if anything - you've got to prove in life?
- Are you scared of dying?
- Do you think you are a lovable person?

- Do you think you are attractive and desirable to others?
- What is your mindset towards life?
- What is your biggest goal, dream or aspiration in life?
- If you had children, what is the number one thing you would teach them?

I passionately believe that we all need to take time to ask ourselves these kinds of introspective questions! See it as your own DIY therapy session, enjoyed from the comfort of your own home!

Here's the thing: **The more you learn about yourself, the more you'll be able to enjoy an enlightened and enriching existence!**

Self-awareness means we stop sleepwalking through life. Remember, **the unexamined life is not worth living!**

When we start to work out who we really are and what we really want in life, we can start working hard to turn our dreams and desires into our reality!

It is only when we start to identify our biggest fears and anxieties that we can start to take the positive steps to overcome them! How many of us find we keep going around in circles and making the same mistakes again and again?

If only we could see where we keep going wrong and then take the steps to improve the quality of our lives! If only we could start to realise the subconscious desires and fears that are driving our actions, and then get proactive about overcoming them!

Well, guess what? We can! When we cultivate self-awareness,

we are able to liberate ourselves from self-created suffering and start creating a more positive life for ourselves instead!

I passionately believe that the secret to making the most of life is choosing to wake up and start cultivating some real self-awareness.

◆ ◆ ◆

To become genuinely happy human beings, we need to get supremely confident in our own skin. **The secret to achieving this confidence is making a conscious effort to start working out exactly who we are.**

Don't be scared about what 'uncomfortable home truths' you might find out – no matter how deep your fears or flaws, you will always have unconditional value and worth! Take time to find out what makes you a unique individual. Stop burying your head in the sand and start embracing who you authentically are!

Spend time getting to know your authentic self. Start working out what things really make you tick, and start identifying which situations always seem to fill you with terror.

This process of introspection is the most empowering and enlightening thing that you can ever do! Remember this: knowing yourself is the beginning of all wisdom!

29. INVEST IN YOURSELF

"The best investment you will ever make is in yourself" (Warren Buffet)

How do you expect to become the best version of your**self without the investment of any time, effort or energy?**

In order to fulfil our potential, find happiness and genuinely flourish in life, it is essential that we invest in ourselves! As pop sensation Jennifer Lopez once said, **to be successful in life you've got to 'work harder than anybody else!'** And let's keep it real - becoming the best version of yourself requires a LOT of hark work and investment!

I'm sorry to be the bearer of bad news, but there is no overnight quick-fix solution to finding happiness and success in life! Instead, you need to think about cultivating success in life in the same way that you would think about building a business empire. You cannot build your successful business without the investment of time, effort and money! In the same way, **you cannot hope to be enjoy success in your personal life or fulfil your potential as a human being without making some serious investments in yourself!**

You need to make your wellbeing your new number 1 priority! As the supermodel Elle Macpherson said in a recent interview: **"Wellness enables people to exude confidence, strength and charisma, to radiate natural vitality, no matter**

what their age. It's this inner vitality that people find attractive".

With this in mind, I wanted to share with you some of my 'top-tips' for investing in yourself. *By putting these ideas into practice, I hope that you will be able to start truly thriving through life:*

• <u>**Know what you want in life**</u> – Setting goals is essential for living a fulfilling life. In order to live your best life, you need to establish exactly what it is that you want from life! Your goal might be related to your career, your family life, a country you want to visit or the person you want to become. Put together a bucket list of all the things that you want to achieve in your life. Try to think about what kind of person you would like to become. Ask yourself this: What does it mean to be YOU? What things are most important in YOUR life? What values do YOU care about the most? When you get to grips with who you are and what you want, you find that life becomes so much more fulfilling and enjoyable. So make sense of who you are and find your place in the world!

• <u>**Invest in your appearance**</u> – take care of your appearance. Invest in a good wardrobe, including a selection of 'power outfits' that make you feel amazing when you wear them. I find that a good pair of skinny jeans, smart trousers and a blazer always makes me feel like I am ready for business. I find that tight fit clothes make me feel empowered and ready to face the world – do not wear anything that makes you feel lazy, slouchy or like you are blending into the background. If you're wearing a bin bag, don't be surprised when people start filling your life with rubbish! Dress for success! The same goes for your skincare and hair style – invest in looking as healthy and attractive as you can. Look after your skin and keep your hair looking fabulous! Looking good isn't just about what other people will think of you – it's about how you feel about yourself! When you invest in your personal appearance, you feel empowered and amazing in your own skin. Looking good means you start feeling good and attract nothing but good things into your life!

• **Eat good food** – There's a famous saying that 'you are what you eat'. Whilst I don't think this is quite literally the case, I do believe that the food you eat has a massive impact on how you feel about yourself. If you are constantly eating unhealthy food, you will obviously feel unhealthy in yourself. You end up feeling lethargic, tired, unmotivated and lacking in self-control. To feel well, we have to eat well. I try to stick to a pretty Mediterranean diet – lots of salads and fresh fruit – because I find this makes me feel most energised, healthy and alive! Find your 'feel good foods'. By this, I do not mean comfort foods that provide a short-term emotional comfort. Rather, I mean the foods that make you feel fabulous, leave your skin glowing and your body fuelled. We want to eat food that shows we respect ourselves and want to care for ourselves – as St Paul writes, your body is a temple of the Holy Spirit! So make it your mission to only eat 'soul food' – that's food that boosts your mood and brightens your day! When it comes to 'soul food', I really do believe that 'the brighter the better' – by this, I mean food that is fresh, vibrant and bursting with goodness! Consume as much 'soul food' as you can – we should strive to eat anything that provides us with vitamins, energy and leaves us feeling ready to face the day! Also, it's important to remember the golden rule I learnt from my granny: 'a little bit of what you fancy does you good!' You need to regularly treat yourself and ensure that you enjoy a balanced diet! In the same way that an overly indulgent diet is bad for your body, an obsessively controlled diet is toxic for your health and wellbeing!

• **Do things that make you happy** – Every day you must spend time doing little things that bring you genuine happiness. You need time where you switch off from your career, your finances, your social media and all the other pressures of modern life – take some 'me' time when you can really unwind and relax. This might be reading a good book, taking a long bath, going for a nice walk or having a coffee with an old friend. We need this daily time for relaxation in order to re-charge – you cannot be at the top of your game if you have no energy left in the tank! When you look after yourself, you invest in yourself!

• **Write in a journal every single day –** This is a simply daily practice that I guarantee will transform your life. Get yourself a notebook or exercise book, or even just go to the notes section on your phone! Get into the habit of writing down your thoughts at either the beginning or end of each day. Sit down and just write whatever is on your mind – express your true thoughts, fears and feelings on the page. Don't think about it – just do it. See this as a daily exercise in therapy and as an opportunity to release all the thoughts and feelings that have been swirling around in your head. I find journaling is my essential daily source of therapy – it gives me so much self-awareness and provides me with so much stress relief. Just getting those words down on the page is the biggest weight off your shoulders and is the best way to start understanding who you authentically are! All that's required is a pen and some paper – and a commitment to taking those 20 minutes a day for a bit of journaling and self-reflection!

• **Get moving everyday –** You need to get up, get out and get moving! Whether it's a 30 minute walk every morning or a 15-minute yoga session after work each night, do something that gets you outside and gets your whole body moving! We need to love our bodies and take care of our physical health – your body should be treated with respect, love and care...too many people abuse themselves by mistreating their bodies! Get moving and get those endorphins pumping – getting proactive is the most positive thing we can do!

• **Read something new every day** – Education is everything! Knowledge is power! The secret to success in this world is committing yourself to learning from every single day of your life! The whole world is your classroom, and every day is an opportunity to grow by discovering new things and becoming the best version of yourself! This all starts with reading. I don't care what it is that you read – an autobiography, a poem, a self-help book, a blog, a news article on your phone…all that matters is that you read SOMETHING every day! We need to stimulate our brains and make time for reflection in our day… the best way to invest in yourself is to read something new every single day! Keep learning, keep growing – and you will find that you start absolutely glowing. Knowledge really is power, you can NEVER learn too many skills – so pick up that book, newspaper or blog post…and get learning!

• **Work on your social skills** - Make time everyday to work on your social skills and your ability to communicate. People seem to assume that you are either born as a 'people person' or a 'socially awkward introvert'. This is absolutely not true! We all have the potential to become skilled communicators and confident conversationalists – it really all comes down to practice and preparation! Make time each day to invest in improving your social confidence and your conversational skills! Start a conversation with the person who serves you in the shop! Read up on the latest news stories of the day so that you can discuss them with a friend! Think of interesting questions you can ask when you're next out for dinner with someone! Social skills are not handed to you on a plate – you need to practice and prepare! Investing in your communication skills is an essential investment in yourself. Becoming an expert at communication is absolutely essential for enjoying real success in this world!

• **Meditate, meditate, meditate!** Of course, I'm evangelising about meditation! Committing to daily meditation is the best kind of investment you can make in yourself! It is the most positive and life-affirming practice. It cultivates gratitude, grounding and enables you to live a genuinely authentic life. Just 20 minutes of meditation a day is sufficient to transform your life – you are able to transcend suffering and connect with your higher purpose in life. Inner peace, genuine confidence and a fulfilling life are all accessible to us right here and now – if only we will give ourselves some space to breathe through the practice of meditation!

Let's get something straight: **Success in life starts with investing in yourself.** So be passionate about taking care of your body, mind, and soul! **Living your best life does not happen by accident – it requires hard work, perserverance and - of course - investment every single day of your life!** Remember, happiness is just as much about enjoying the journey as it is about reaching a final destination! So fall in love with the process of investing in yourself...and start thriving through life!

30. THE IMPORTANCE OF SELF LOVE

"You're always with yourself, so you might as well enjoy the company!" (Diane Von Furstenburg)

If you can't love yourself then how on earth are you going to love anybody else?

I passionately believe that **the solid foundation for a fearless life is self-love.**

You cannot be happy in your life if you do not unconditionally love and accept who you authentically are. **By anchoring yourself in this self -acceptance and love, you are able to arm yourself with the confidence and resilience required to go out into this world and live your best life!** All success in your life starts with a radical and complete acceptance of who you authentically are.

Self-love means giving yourself this unconditional acceptance. Self-love is all about liking yourself and loving who you are no matter how many mistakes you make or how many times you get things wrong. Your self-love needs to be totally independent of anything that you do or anything that anybody else says about you.

'Self-love' means thinking and acting like somebody who actually likes themselves. It's all about knowing that you deserve to live a happy, fulfilling, and meaningful life.

Now, this definition of self-love might come as a bit of a surprise to you. Many people seem to assume that self-love is all about selfishly believing you are perfect and delusionally thinking that you are somehow better than everybody else. We hear the words 'self-love' and instantly translate them to mean 'egotistical, self-obsessed and with a very bad God-complex'. This couldn't be further from the truth!

Here's what I believe: the people who look like they are 'self-obsessed' and drowning in their own self-importance are often the ones most lacking in genuine self-love. I believe very strongly that 'confidence is quiet, insecurities are loud'.

Someone with genuine self-love will not be desperate for attention or external validation. They will, of course, enjoy a bit of limelight and a compliment or two. After all, it's only human to desire a little bit of external validation from time to time! But here's the important thing: **someone with genuine self-love will not get all of their validation as a human being from the compliments and attention given to them by others!**

That's because when someone has authentic self-love, **they have a concrete source of validation <u>within them</u>.** They do not feel the need to spend 24 hours a day telling the world how amazing they are and begging for people to pay them attention.

When it appears that someone has too much self-love, the reality is almost always that they actually have far too little. Remember, self-love is not about vanity and needing to constantly be the centre of attention.

Self-love is instead about unconditionally accepting yourself and knowing that you have unconditional worth as a human being. Your worth is not dependent on how much

money you gain or how much attention you have.

Cultivating authentic self-love means realising this uncondi-tional worth and letting go of your obsessions with social sta-tus and popularity. **It's about learning let go of this need for external validation and learning to love yourself instead. You have nothing to prove and no-one that you need to impress.** When we have genuine self-love, **we become genuinely happy in our own skin and totally secure in our identity**.

Self-love really is the greatest revolution. **When you have genuine self-love, anything is possible**. We are finally re-leased from the prison of public opinion and are at last al-lowed to break free from the chains of anxiety and fear.

So, what does living with self-love actually look like? **For a start, it means unconditionally accepting who we authenti-cally are.** In social relationships, it means that we conduct ourselves with kindness and dignity at all times. We conduct ourselves like people who *prefer* to be liked by other people, but don't *depend* on other people's validation in order to feel good about ourselves.

It could not be clearer: **self-love is the essential foundation for living a confident and resilient life.** Having self-love gives you the courage to be disliked by other people, which is vital if you are to free yourself from the prison of public opinion and start living life on your own terms. **Self-love gives you the ability to start taking risks and stepping outside of your comfort zone, because you know that no matter what hap-pens, you can handle it**! And it gives you the ability to develop genuine and meaningful relationships in which you will feel respected, valued and fulfilled.

Remember, **if you can't love yourself then how on earth are you going to love anybody else? Make self-love your new priority in life.**

It's time to get serious about completely accepting the person you authentically are and becoming absolutely sure of your unconditional worth as a human being.

Whilst people and places may come and go, you are your own constant companion throughout life. From the moment we are born until the moment we die, you will be living your life in your own company!

It is essential that we unconditionally like, love, and accept the people we authentically are.

So here's what you need to do:

Stop criticising yourself so harshly.

Stop beating yourself up so mercilessly.

Talk to yourself in the same way that you would talk to a close friend – treat yourself with the kindness and compassion that you deserve.

Aspire to form an honest, authentic, and loving relationship with yourself.

Build your success in life on **the unshakeable foundation of unconditional self-acceptance and self-love (which, at the end of the day, are the same thing).**

And just remember that with genuine self-love, anything really is possible...

31. GRATITUDE LEADS TO GREATNESS

"Acknowledging the good that you already have in your life is the foundation for all abundance" – (Eckhart Tolle)

If there is one practice that has the power to totally transform your life for the better right now, it is gratitude.

When we commit ourselves to living a life of gratitude – which is characterised by the habit of 'counting your blessings' and becoming deeply thankful for every single opportunity that the universe offers to us - we grant ourselves the permission to experience more happiness and fulfilment in our lives than ever before!

In every single area of your life, gratitude is the best medi-

cine. It heals your mind, body and your spirit! Gratitude not only makes us more thankful for everything that we already have in our lives, but it also attracts even more things to be thankful for into our lives!

As I always like to tell people, **gratitude is the great multiplier!** The more you express gratitude, the more goodness you will attract into your life! Without gratitude, happiness in life is quite simply impossible.

Here's the thing: **If we do not live our lives with a deep sense of gratitude, we will never ever feel happy or fulfilled.**

Let me explain: There are many people in this world who continue feeling deeply unfulfilled no matter how much they acquire. They could have millions of pounds in the bank or hundreds of holiday homes around the world, and yet still they feel deeply unhappy inside.

In our world today, there are so many people who are always craving more and are never quite able to find true contentment in life. For these poor souls, nothing is ever enough.

Why are so many people living this kind of unfulfilled and unhappy life? Why do they feel so empty and lost in this world? It is because they are not practicing gratitude. **In order to find true happiness in life, you need to become genuinely thankful for every single blessing that the the universe hands to you.**

Here's the thing that most people never realise: accumulating more will never satisfy you unless you **start genuinely appreciating everything that you already have.**

I firmly believe that **practicing gratitude turns everything you touch into gold. It completely transforms the way we see the world.**

When we start living life with a real sense of gratitude, **our life becomes a gift to be cherished rather than an ordeal to be endured**. Every obstacle becomes an opportunity and every challenge becomes a chance to grow as a human being. With gratitude, **every daily habit that we once found boring and mundane becomes a life-affirming act that brings a little bit of positivity into our day!**

A life of gratitude must start with being thankful for the smallest of things. **It begins with being thankful for the fact that you are alive.** That's right, we must express deep gratitude simply for the fact that we are here on this planet and we are getting to experience this extraordinary phenomenon called life!

Every single human life is a miracle – let's keep it real, you are the most extraordinary organism! Just the fact that you are breathing and thinking is incredible! When you live with gratitude, you see every single day as a gift to be cherished with every single bone in your body!

As Albert Einstein once said, **'there are only two ways to live your life. One is as though nothing is a miracle. The other is as though everything is a miracle'.**

 In life, you just never know what is around the corner – sorry to be morbid, but who knows when you are going to just drop down dead? It's a sobering reminder that **we must genuinely appreciate and fully embrace the gift of every single day, because you really do not know which day is going to be your last.**

Gratitude is all about taking a fresh look at all the 'everyday' things that we all take for granted and breathing a brand new

spirit of appreciation into our lives!

Now, it's important to remember that gratitude doesn't just apply to the good things in your life – we should be thankful for even the most challenging and difficult experiences we have to go through! You never know what challenging experience might in fact turn out to be a 'blessing in disguise'! **We should therefore be thankful for even the most difficult and challenging times in our lives, because it only by going through adversity that we can grow as human beings!**

With this in mind, I wholeheartedly urge you to **start expressing gratitude for every single challenge that life throws at you.** Just remember, **the universe will never present you with a challenge that you cannot handle or that you cannot learn from!**

So you must **be deeply thankful for every single opportunity that the universe gives you!** Remember that you can handle whatever you are going through...and you can even grow through what you go through! *You obviously needed to learn this essential life lesson!*

It is thanks to life's setbacks and struggles that we are able to cultivate character and become the strong, resilient and confident human beings that we all aspire to be. We should therefore appreciate every single piece of adversity that we have been through! Remember my mantra - **you grow through what you go through!**

So be thankful for all of these opportunities to learn and grow! However painful or unfair an experience may seem at the time, when we look back in years to come, *we might just be thankful for the life lessons it has taught us!*

Maybe it's because I aspire to become a school teacher and leader in education, but I like to think of it like this: **We are**

all students at the 'school of life', and we must be immensely thankful for every single lesson that the universe sends to us! Some people say to me that they will only have gratitude once they have got what they want. They claim they're going to 'delay' their gratitude until they have achieved their dreams. Or they say they'll start appreciating the gift of life once they have got through the tough time that they are currently going through.

Whilst I totally understand this mindset, I also have to break it to you that this attitude towards gratitude is absolutely wrong! **We should not wait another single second before we start actively expressing gratitude in every single area of our lives.**

The truth is this - <u>**GRATITUDE STARTS RIGHT HERE!**</u> To provide that point, I challenge you right now to find at least 10 things to be grateful for in your life. Think of the simplest things - it might be the cup of tea that you're holding or the it might be the delicious meal you have for dinner last night.

Gratitude is also a very helpful practice in times of loss and grief. There's a beautiful quote attributed to Dr Seuss that reads - **'Don't cry because it's over, smile because it happened'**. When we make an effort to practice gratitude, we are able to treasure our memories rather than mourn our losses.

When we are grieving the loss of a loved one, for example, gratitude reminds us that 'the loss is immeasurable but so is the love left behind'. In times of sorrow, mourning and less, instead of being angry and upset about what / who you no longer have in your life, **try to express gratitude for what you did have and for the happiness that was brought into your life**. Those memories and that love will never leave you. So you should strive t**o become deeply thankful for what you did have and how this helped you to become more as a human** being, rather than being angry about what you are no longer able to enjoy.

All good things must come to an end. Every single human being is born and then must die. We cannot dwell the loss of an experience, an opportunity or a loved one - we must instead cherish our memories and express gratitude for the opportunities that we were so blessed to be able to enjoy.

Everywhere we look, there is so much to appreciate! Look at the world with a genuine spirit of gratitude, and find that *everything in your life turns to gold!*

Just because you don't have everything you want right now, that doesn't mean you cannot practice gratitude right now. In fact, John Candy once said this: **"If you're not happy without it, you'll never be happy with it".**

Gratitude is the secret to finding genuine happiness, contentment and fulfilment in life. It is your golden ticket to living your very best life, and is a guaranteed way of making everything you touch turn to gold.

When we have gratitude for both the smallest pleasures and the biggest of challenges in our lives, we are able to transform our entire existence. That's why it's so important that we tart appreciating every single day and every single opportunity that we have on this planet!

Remember - **it is only when we start practicing gratitude that we will start attracting even more things to be grateful for into our lives!** Gratitude is the great multiplier! So, what are you waiting for?

START LOOKING AT THE WORLD WITH AN ATTITUDE OF APPRECIATION AND START TURNING EVERYTHING THAT YOU TOUCH INTO GOLD!

32. GET YOUR PRIORITIES RIGHT

"The key is not to prioritise what's on your schedule, but to schedule your priorities" (Stephen Covey)

Imagine that you had to name the five most important things in your life right now – what would they be?

I want you to take a moment to consider this very important question: what are the most important things in your life? What do you value the most in your life? In our busy lives, we all seem to always have a million more things that we need to get done.

Every day can start to seem like a constant struggle to keep up, with all these different tasks to be done. We could spend our lives drowning in endless lists of 'things to do' and exhaust ourselves working every hour in the day trying to get all of these tasks done.

But what is it all for? Why are we slaving away seven days a week to get all of these supposedly 'important' jobs done? We need to establish what we're doing all this hard work for. Never mind getting all these trivial and menial tasks done – what is the bigger picture and bigger purpose behind your life?

We need to stop wasting our precious time and energy worrying about petty things and start focusing on the things that are truly important in our lives!

Living a life filled with purpose starts with getting your priorities right.

What matters most to you in your life? What things do you care about the most? What people, activities and pursuits bring your life a real sense of meaning?

Once you have established what things are most important in your life, you should not think twice before investing every single drop of energy you have into them!

Your time and energy are so precious. Only invest them in things that really matter to you. In other words, stop worrying about things that are absolutely irrelevant to your life! Stop feeling bad about putting your family, friends, faith or mental health first – if something is important to you, then you need to start making it an absolute priority in your life.

Never feel bad for being assertive about your priorities. You cannot live your life as a people pleaser who is trying to be all things to all people at all times! You need to take ownership of your own life and start using your time wisely! **Don't let yourself get distracted by pointless problems and trivial tasks! At all times, keep your focus on doing more of the things that will bring you genuine fulfilment in life.**

It is not enough to just know what your priorities are - you need to get serious about doing something practical with them!

You need to start setting yourself intelligent goals and ambitious targets that will allow you to do more of the things that bring you genuine happiness. If, for example, family is the most important thing in your life, ten try to set yourself clear goals about spending more time with your family. Make an effort to set some achievable targets to do with investing more energy into strengthening those family relationships.

Your goals should be set based on the 'SMART TARGET' model. This model allows us to set clear and concise targets we can work towards achieving in our lives. This allows us to be extraordinarily efficient at fulfilling our dreams and doing more of the things that give our lives meaning.

A SMART TARGET should be made up of five key components:

S – Specific. It should be specific, for example 'I will make an effort to call my parents once a week' or 'I will make an effort to spend more time with my family, starting with organising a family meal'

M – Measurable. You need to be able to check whether you are successfully meeting your target and achieving your goals. For example, saying that you will call your parents once a week is measurable – you can tick it off each week you achieve it

A – Achievable. Keep your targets realistic! Whilst 'bring about world peace' is a noble aim, it is not something one person can achieve in one week! Start with achievable targets, such as that you will write a blog post on why non-violence is important or by joining an organisation working for world peace

R – Relevant. Your target needs to be relevant to your overall purpose in life! Why is family so important to you in life? Why do you care so much about working for world peace? Make sure your target fits with your world view and connects with your core values in life.

T – Time-Based. If we want to get productive about our priorities, we need to make our targets time-based. There's no point going through life with broad aspirations and general intentions – you will end up never getting anything done! To turn your dreams into your reality, you need to set time-

based targets! Break your big dreams down into manageable chunks and achievable challenges, and you will start seeing the most amazing results in your life!

In summary, it is so important that you know are clear about your priorities in life and that you get SMART about setting targets designed to facilitate flourishing in these areas!

Your time is precious, so it is essential that you use it wisely! Living your best life starts with being clear about your priorities. **Stop wasting your precious time worrying about problems and situations that do not matter!** Instead, focus that precious time and energy on the things that are genuinely important to you.

This is your one life – stop sweating the small stuff and start living it to the full!

33. DON'T THINK ABOUT IT, JUST DO IT

"Don't overthink it. Go out and do it" (Ben Wardle)

If there's one mantra I repeat more than any other, it's this: feel the fear...and do it anyway! We need to stop letting feelings fear and anxiety rule our lives! We need to stop holding back or avoiding situations because we are scared of what might happen. In other words: don't think about it, **JUST DO IT!**

If you do not take control of your worries, your worries will start to control your whole entire life. **Your thoughts are here to help you – they should never be given so much power that they are able to start limiting you!**

I think it's time for a bit of breaking news: **you do not have to be a slave to your anxieties or a servant to your fears for a single second longer!** That's right, if you want to achieve something or if you want to do something, then why on earth are you continuing to let your anxious thoughts and feelings of fear hold you back!

I strongly believe that fear exists for one purpose: to be conquered. And the only way to conquer fear is to JUST GO OUT AND DO the things that scare you the most!

You have quite simply got to just take the plunge and fear-

lessly put yourself out there.

Boldly step outside of your comfort zone and throw yourself into doing the things that scare you the most!

 The trick is this: don't let yourself think about it, because the more you dwell on it in your mind, the most likely you are to end up talking yourself out of it! To overcome your fears, you've got to start learning to feel the fear...and do it anyway!

Every single day, make it your mission to do another thing that scares you. That might be starting a conversation with the cashier in the shop or it might be stepping out in a piece of clothing that you're scared people will laugh at you for wearing. **Make a habit of boldly stepping outside of your comfort zone. Get absolutely addicted to feeling the fear!**

If you want to grow and thrive through life, then you need to get busy overcoming your fears. You need to get out there and do more the things that scare you the most! Every single day you need to make it your mission to *feel the fear...and do it anyway.*

Living your best life does not happen inside your comfort zone. You need to break free of your fears and boldly step outside of your protective bubbles. **Life is not about staying safe – when we stick to what we know, we never get a chance to grow.**

Keep in mind that whatever happens, you can handle it. Remind yourself that even the worst-case outcome is better than letting fear impose limitations on your life yet again.

Take those risks, put yourself out there – and start thriving through life! You grow through what you go through – and you can't grow if you don't do anything that really scares you!

Once you become fearless, you become limitless.

Start living your best life by learning to feel the fear...and do it anyway.

Get out there, remember how strong you are...and JUST DO IT!

34. STRIVE TO BE INTERESTED, NOT INTERESTING

"Every single person you meet in your life has an important lesson to teach you. Stop worrying about what they think of you and start listening to what they have to say" (Ben Wardle)

I want to start by asking you this question: **How do you become a popular, magnetic, and truly likeable person?**

I very strongly believe that it all comes down to just one thing. This is another one of my Biblical commandments for living your very best life (get this one added to the fridge magnet collection right now!)! Here it is:

in every social situation, <u>you should strive to take an real interest in other people, rather than worrying about whether you appear interesting to them.</u>

To put it another way; **if you want to actually become interesting in life, then you've got to focus on becoming interested in other people!**

In his bestselling and revolutionary self-help book 'How to Win Friends and Influence People', Dale Carnegie shares all-important law of human conduct. According to Carnegie, following this law will not only keep us out of trouble but will also bring us countless friends and constant happiness. So what is his Biblical rule for social success? It is this:

Always make the other person feel important.

The philosopher William James would have agreed with this golden rule for social success, having written in the 19th century that the **'deepest principle in human nature is the craving to be appreciated'**.

Here's the thing: **absolutely everybody wants to feel important. It's in our DNA as human beings!** And so when you aspire to become someone who is an expert at making people feel important, you start to become extraordinarily important yourself!

I therefore believe that in life, **you should strive to become someone who makes people feel valued and important!** Make it your mission to become *that* somebody who empowers people and brings a bit of sunshine into their day!

The guaranteed way of making somebody feel important is **taking a genuine interest in them.** Show that you genuinely care about what is going on in their life and ask about how they are feeling today. **Validate what they say to you. Ask questions that will allow them to talk at length about the subjects they are most interested in!**

When you take this active interest in someone, you are saying to them **'YOU ARE IMPORTANT'**. This is Disney-level magic! It is like sprinkling gold dust all over them and carrying them on a throne!

When you become someone who is able to make people feel good about themselves – by showing them that you are genu-

inely interested in what they have to say – you bring nothing but good things into your own life as well!

You should therefore **make it your mission to make every single person you meet feel important and good about themselves.** The easiest way to do this is by becoming genuinely interested in what everybody has to say. When you genuinely listen to someone and take an active interest in them, *you make them feel a million dollars*!

In order to enjoy social success, you must start to realise that **'the royal road to a person's heart is to talk about the things he or she treasures most'.** As Disraeli once said,

'Talk to people about themselves and they will listen for hours'.

When you start a conversation, **think in terms of the other person's interests.** What topics are they most passionate about? What topics will they be desperate to talk to you about? What things might they want to tell you about?

In order to find this out, you should look for clues in what the other person is wearing (for example, give them a sincere compliment about their outfit) or find out what they have been doing that day (for example, are they carrying anything that would give away a hobby or interest that they are passionate about?). **Use these 'hooks' to ask people questions that show a genuine interest in their life.**

The fact is this: <u>**Nothing makes somebody feel more important than another human being taking a genuine interest in them.**</u> Even a simple 'hello' can make someone feel a million dollars! Become someone who makes people feel important about themselves, and you will find that you become a very popular, respected, and powerful person indeed!

Dale Carnegie wrote this: **"I have discovered from personal experience that one can win the attention and time and co-operation of even the most sought-after people by becoming genuinely interested in them".**

Most of the time, we are all in competition for attention. There is a never-ending battle for airtime in conversation, with everyone trying to prove how amazing they are. **People are desperate to appear interesting and to win approval for their achievements.** The problem is this - desperate just isn't a good look! Any attempts to gain approval for your achievements can very easily look like attention-seeking.

The secret to becoming a genuinely interesting person is therefore not to try and look interesting. You should actually try to do the opposite - you should strive to become genuinely <u>interested</u> in other people.

To put it another way, **you should not be worrying about how you can impress other people but instead be working out how we can show a genuine interest in them**.

I like to think of it like this: you have two ears and one mouth, and you should use them in that proportion! **In conversation, you should spend 75% of your time listening to what the other person has to say.** And when I say listening, I mean genuinely listening! **Show someone that you genuinely care about what they are saying and I guarantee that they will show you loyalty and kindness in return!**

Don't ask 'how can I make myself look important in this situation?' Don't ask 'how am I going to impress people and make myself look good today?' Instead ask **'What can I do to make the people I meet feel important about themselves?**

How can I show them that I value them and think that they

are important?

What can I do to make their day that little bit better?'

It all starts with a strong smile, strong eye contact and a 'hello, how are you?' **Give each person you meet your full attention and take a genuine interest in them and what they have to say. Genuinely take an interest in how their day is going and seek to bring a bit of sunshine into their lives!**

When you take a genuine interest in other people, you bring nothing but goodness back into your own life. Know the rule: **if you want to be interesting, you've got to focus on becoming interested in everyone you meet.**

So what are you waiting for? Get out there, ask questions, listen to people's answers...**and make them feel a million dollars!**

35. ALWAYS ACT LIKE YOU ARE LIKED

"Whenever you go outside, draw the chin in, carry the crown of the head high, and fill the lungs to the utmost; drink in the sunshine, greet your friends with a smile, and put soul into every handshake. Do not fear being misunderstood and do not waste a minute thinking about your enemies. Try to fix firmly in your mind what you would like to do; and then, without veering off direction, you will move straight to the goal. Keep your mind on the great and splendid things you would like to do, and then, as the days go gliding away, you will find yourself unconsciously seizing upon the opportunities that are a requirement for the fulfilment of your desires..." (Elbert Hubbard)

Social confidence is as simple as this: act as though everybody in the world likes you. That's not to say that they do, because it's a fact of life that you can never please everyone – and should never try to!

But what it does mean is that **you should enter every social situation believing that people will most-probably like you and knowing that if they do not, you will be able to handle that fact!**

◆ ◆ ◆

When it comes to social confidence, I believe very strongly in **the importance of maintaining a positive mental attitude.**

When we act like somebody who likes themselves, we are very likeable in the eyes of other people. On the other hand, when we act like somebody who expects to be judged and disliked by other people, they instantly pick up on this and we will end up turning our biggest fears of rejection into a self-fulfilling prophecy.

Think about it: **if you go into a social situation expecting people to dislike you, how will this affect your entire body language and mood?** Your negative mindset will take over you – you will spend the whole evening anticipating rejection, ridicule, and negative judgment. Both your body language and conversation will be anxious and defensive.

You'll be actively looking around to find someone who will dislike you! As a result of your defensiveness and anxiety, people will struggle to warm to you and will feel uncomfortable when they are around you. Your fear of being disliked will therefore turn into a self-fulfilling prophecy!

On the other hand, if you go into a social situation expecting people to like you, think about how this instantly improves your body language and mood! With this positive mindset, you will spend the whole evening putting other people at ease, entering into interesting conversations, and having the time of your life.

Your body language and conversation will exude nothing but self-confidence and charisma.

You will become magnetic – people are instantly attracted to those who 'light up a room' and radiate effortless charm.

There is again a self-fulfilling prophecy, but this time it is a very positive one – because you expected to be liked, you behaved in a likeable way...**and so people did indeed like you!** *insert round of applause and set off a confetti cannon here*

This all comes down to your self-confidence and your self-image. **You have to believe deep down that you are a genuinely likeable person.**

Here's the Biblical truth of social interaction: **In order to thrive in social situations you must <u>at all times keep your vibration positive and your self-confidence high!</u>**

I strongly believe that we need to stop seeing social events as assessments of our worth or likeability as human beings! The vast majority of people do not go out looking for people to criticise and judge – they go out wanting to do exactly the same thing as you, which is to make friends and have a good time! They are usually feeling just as anxious and apprehensive about socialising as you are...some people are just a lot better at faking it and pretending that they're not!

This is where my number one tip of all time comes in... **in every social situation, you must always keep your focus on the other person and not on you.** Let me explain: When you're in conversation, don't focus on whether your body language is correct or if that person actually likes you. **Instead, keep your whole entire focus on making the other person feel comfortable and at ease**.

Here's how it works: in your head, don't worry for one second about how you look or how you are coming across. Instead, **focus all of your attention on the other person – carefully listen to what they are saying and consider the ways in which you can make them feel more at ease and comfortable.**

Instead of scrutinising yourself, keep your focus on putting the other person at ease.

The chances are that the person you are talking to is just as nervous about this social interaction as you are! If it doesn't look like they are, then just assume that they are just doing a much better job of hiding it than you are!

Don't worry about whether this person actually likes you or not. Instead, **simply just assume that they do like you...and notice how confident you instantly become!** Then safe in the assumption that your conversational partner likes you, **you can put all of your focus on having a good time making conversation to them!** *Stop worrying and start working that room!*

This is a win-win strategy, because it not only ensures you present yourself as both attractive and likeable, but it also stops anxiety and insecurity from internally consuming you!

I like think of it like this – **even if the person you are dealing with doesn't like you, you should still aspire to conduct yourself with kindness and dignity.** *So you might as well assume that they DO like you, even if they have made it very clear that they do not!*

Remember, **what other people think of you is none of your business!** I could not care less about whether you like me or not! But what I do care about is presenting myself as somebody who actually likes themselves and feels completely confident in their own skin.

I want to be known as somebody who conducts themselves with kindness and dignity at all times. That means treating people - even those who don't like me - with that kindness and dignity... at all times!

Don't give someone who doesn't like you the satisfaction of lowering your vibe! Instead, simply **Expect to be liked and you will find that this becomes a self-fulfilling prophecy**!

With your positive mental attitude and your commitment to putting other people at ease, you are socially unstoppable.

Remember, genuinely confident people expect to be liked but have no absolutely no problem coping if they're not.

Get confident in your own skin! Stop worrying and start working the room!

Own every single social situation that you find yourself in - take control of your fears and become a fabulous social conversationalist!

Stop seeing social interactions as a test of your likeability and start seeing them as opportunities to have a bit of fun!

Stop worrying about what other people think about you and start assuming that they do indeed like you.

Allow this 'positive social mindset' to truly transform your social life! And remember, keep your vibration positive and your self-confidence high! It's your time to shine!

36. THE 'MEET & GREET MINDSET'

"In a world filled with instant coffee, aspire to become a sparkling bottle of champagne" (Ben Wardle)

We're going to stick with the theme of making people feel like a million dollars now, because I now want to unveil my number 1 secret weapon for social success. My dear reader, I present to you the 'MEET & GREET MINDSET!'

Back when I was 17, I had the time of my life working at a 120-room 5* hotel. My job was to 'meet and greet' the guests as they arrived at the main reception desk, welcoming them in and guiding them around the hotel. It was my role to make them feel welcomed and to ensure that their stay was smooth from start to finish.

It was also my role to help guests by carrying their luggage up the flights of stairs - however, as I'm sure you can imagine, this part of the job was not exactly my area of expertise (or enthusiasm)...

On early morning shifts I would say 'good morning!' and direct my guests to the restaurant for breakfast, whilst on a Friday night, I would point guests to the Champagne Bar or book them a taxi into Manchester.

My absolutely favourite shift of the week was a Saturday,

when 200 wedding guests would arrive at the hotel, each receiving a glass of Prosecco as they walked down the red carpet and through the main reception doors. They would all spend hours posing for pictures in the 270 acres of land around the hotel, perfecting the best Instagram poses and showing their glamorous wedding outfits off to the world. As I'm sure you can imagine, I absolutely loved the buzz of welcoming all these people into the hotel, doing what I could to add a little bit of sparkle to their stay.

Getting this incredible job was the best thing that could have ever happened to 17-year-old me. It was literally like divine intervention - it came at just the right time and completely transformed my entire life! It gave me the most amazing people skills and the most extraordinary boost of confidence that I will forever be thankful for.

During my time in this fabulous job, I devised what I now like to call the 'meet & greet mindset' (as you should know by now, I'm very extra like that!) This mindset is the secret weapon that I deploy in every single social situation that I face in my life today! And I hope that it might be able to help *you* out in terms of your social confidence as well…

So what is my 'meet & greet mindset'? All me to explain! In every social situation, I imagine that I am back at work standing in the main entrance door to the hotel.

With the click of my fingers, I instantly snap back into the role of being 'host with the most'!

I remind myself that it is my job to warmly welcome every single person that I see and that it is my job to make sure that every single person that I interact with feels at ease. It is my job – which I am being paid to do, and so I must be at the very top of my game at all times – to make eye contact, plaster on my biggest smile, and give every person I meet the warmest greeting that I can muster.

It doesn't matter if I'm scared of what someone might think about me or whether I fear that someone might potentially end up being dismissive of my friendliness – **it is my JOB to say hello and to ask them how they are!**

In my first few weeks in the job, I remember feeling so much anxiety about having to speak to certain groups of people. I'd see people – usually groups of men – who I assumed would mock me or ridicule me. As a result of my insecurities and fears, I would instantly assume that they wouldn't want to engage with my attempts at making conversation. I expected that they would make comments to each other about how 'gay' I was, or even start doing nasty impressions of how I spoke. And so when these groups of people walked towards the entrance to the hotel - where I was waiting to greet everyone that arrived - it literally felt like all of my worst nightmares coming true...and quite literally walking straight towards me! My heart would start racing and my palms would start sweating.

In those moments of overwhelming panic and anxiety, I could quite easily have run away from the door and have pretended that I'd never seen those 'fearsome' guests arriving. I could have quite easily slipped off for a quick toilet break, or made myself look busy organising local attraction leaflets in the champagne bar.

But that wasn't what I stood for as an employee. 17-year old me took my commitment to delivering 5* service very seriously indeed! I therefore knew that I had to pull myself together and realise that this situation wasn't about me.

I was here to do a job, and do that job was exactly what I was going to do! It did not matter what these people thought of me - my job was to meet and greet them, and I was going to give them the meet and greet of their lives!

I had to realise that I wasn't standing here in the hotel foyer in order to be subjected to an assessment of my character or to face an appraisal of my personality!

No, I was here to do my job - which I loved more than anything else - and I was committed to doing it in STYLE! And so I made it my mission to not let my fears and anxieties hold me back from delivering that full 5* service!

I therefore allowed myself to acknowledge those feelings of anxiety - and they really did make me want to run a mile - but I then forced myself to stoically remain routed to the spot! I was not going to be defeated by my fears - I was going to 'fake it until I made it' instead!

And so instead of running away from the door as these scary groups of people approached, I forced myself to make eye contact, plaster on my biggest smile, and give those guests the warmest welcome that I could! I didn't let myself think about it for one second - I simply got into character and got down to business!

I greeted all of those intimidating guests with a massive smile and a cheerful 'Hi, how are you today?' or a 'Hello, good evening...welcome to Mottram Hall!' I completely faked my confidence and I completely concealed all of my fears and insecurities.

 Looking at me, any of these guests would have assumed that I was the most confident person on the face of the earth. They had absolutely no idea whatsoever that I was secretly terrified on the inside!

And guess what? The 'fake it till you make it' approach 100%

paid off!

Every single time that I made myself snap into character and fake this social confidence, I found that it got easier and easier.

I soon realised that these guests didn't all start attacking and mocking me right before my own very eyes. I found that instead, they responded to my friendliness with...guess what... FRIENDLINESS!!!

I couldn't believe it!! And so I no longer needed to fake my social confidence - I now had genuine confidence and an absolute love for every aspect of my job!

Of course, there were always that tiny minority of guests who would exchange a judgemental glance with one another, but I was determined not to let it phase me. It was my job to greet them...and greet them I would! I was no longer faking my social confidence - I was radiating a genuine love for meeting & greeting new people!

I was being paid to do it, after all, and 17 year old me wanted all that dollar! I was determined to be a true professional and become the dazzling King – or should that be Queen – of the meet and greet!

And so I got into the habit of swallowing my anxieties, face down my social fears, and plastering on my brightest smile.

My 'meet & greet mindset' technique worked absolute wonders.

Each time that I went through the 'meet & greet' motions', I found that talking to people became easier and easier!

It became second nature to make eye contact, plaster on a dazzling smile, and exchange those small talk pleasantries. Meeting & greeting became something that I didn't even need to think about before doing – every single guest would automatically receive what I soon self-titled the 'FIVE STAR BEN WARDLE EXPERIENCE'.

I saw myself as a character in a Disneyland parade, who was being paid to make dreams come true by spreading a little sparkle and joy in people's days.

And whilst my lovely suit was not quite a Mickey Mouse costume, it felt like my battle armour!

And so every time that I got ready for work, I'd get myself straight back into character as Mr Meet & Greet.

In my head, I was this beaming and beautifully bronzed (I was in the middle of a fake tan addiction) host with the most, who always had a bottle of champagne in hand and with a confetti canon exploding above my head.

When I was in this mindset, I truly believed that every single thing that I touched instantly turned into gold and that every person I met was instantly made to feel like a multi-millionaire VIP.

And this meet & greet mindset soon started helping me out in other areas of my life as well. At sixth form college, for example, I started confidently gliding down the corridors and making small talk about the weather with anyone who I encountered!

When I went into Tesco, I'd not only buy my newspapers and meal deal but I would also now have a good chat with the staff and tell them to 'have a great day!'

At parties, which had previously filled me with so much anxiety and fear, I now entered the room safe in the knowledge that I was this fabulous 'Mr Meet & Greet'! I was confident that making people feel at ease and spreading a bit of sparkle was something I was an expert at - I had nothing to fear and had no reason to feel intimidated!

As with everything in life, practice really did make perfect when it came to deploying my 'Meet & Greet' mindset! The more I'd chat to people, make small talk and get into the mindset of being this fabulous host with the most, the easier it would become to talk to anyone! I really do believe that charisma, confidence and charm can easily be cultivated through regular practice!

And as I got more and more confident in my 'meet & greet' mindset, I was starting to give Kris Jenner a run for her money! These days, I'd quite happily make conversation with a brick wall - and it's all because of my meet & greet mindset!

I still deploy this trusted mindset in every social situation today. And so can you! When I walk into a room, I strive to provide that 'BW 5* EXPERIENCE' to every single person I encounter!

 There are no excuses for not acknowledging someone or starting a conversation – see it as your my job to talk to everyone!

 Think of yourself as a professional socialite or an expert host with the most! With this attitude, it is so much easier to get over those inevitable feelings of awkwardness and anxiety that we all feel when entering a social situation!

It really is so simple – you just tell yourself 'IT IS MY JOB TO BE A PROFESSIONAL AND GIVE EVERY SINGLE PERSON THAT I MEET THE FULL 'MEET & GREET' EXPERIENCE!'

I like to tell myself that the people I encounter in my daily life are just like the paying guests I had to look after at work. Even though the people I encounter in the street or at a party are obviously not paying guests, it does me no harm to hold this keep in my mind – it ensures that I am constantly at the top of the social skills game and that I am constantly giving everybody that I encounter the meet & greet experience of their lives!

I don't care whether they love me or can't stand me - as far as I am concerned, I am Mr Meet & Greet...and I am bloody good at my job! I think of it like this: who wouldn't love someone it if someone made them feel like a million dollars?

An important thing that you need to know about the Meet & Greet mindset is that there is no such thing as a day off! At work, it wouldn't matter what time of morning I started – or what time I had gone to bed the night before – I was always committed to being totally on top of my game. I saw myself as like a member of cabin crew on a glamorous airline (I liked to think First Class British Airways or Virgin Atlantic, thank you very much!) Up in the air, normal time went straight out of the window – no matter the time of the day, it is ALWAYS SHOWTIME!

And do even if I had endured the worst week in the world or was feeling a little worse-for-wear from the night before (and I did turn 18 during my time in this job, don't forget!), I would always make sure I got straight into role at work and consistently devlivered that full meet & greet experience!

It was my JOB and I had to be a professional providing that full meet and greet package to every single person that I saw!

Even if it was 6am or I was 16 hours into a shift, I always made sure that I'd had my green tea and that I consistently provided that sparkling 5* level of service! *Looking back, I must admit that it did help to keep a lot of sugar and a lot of concealer in close proximity at all times!*

Start applying the 'Meet & Greet mindset' to your social life and reap the rewards! **Become the host with the most** and the **5* greeter** that you were born to be! **Give everyone eye contact, an award-winning smile, and some seriously smooth small talk. Make everyone feel a million dollars – and stop worrying about what they think of you!**

You've got a job to do – so spread some sparkle and give people the 5* treatment that they deserve!

Get into the meet & greet mindset and get out into the world...*you are the host with the most, and this is your time to shine!*

37. HOW TO TALK TO ANYBODY

"The most attractive thing you can ever wear is confidence" (Ben Wardle)

Strangers are just friends you haven't met yet. Every single person that you meet in this world has the potential to absolutely transform your life!

You never know what one smile or one 5-minute conversation could end up leading to. One minute you could be standing behind someone in the queue at Tesco, the next minute you could be getting married to them and raising six children together! I therefore believe that as you go through life, you should make it your mission to start as many meaningful conversations with as many different people as you possibly can!

I see starting conversation as a bit like the fairground game hook-a-duck - you're going to win a prize every single! Starting conversations everywhere you go is always a winning formula for social success! In every social situation, look for new opportunities to make small talk and get to know new people. Seize every single chance that you get to do a good bit of networking!

Remember, you really do never know what doors your next conversation could open!

<u>Every single person we meet has the potential to teach us something extremely important.</u> Even if somebody is rude, nasty or judgemental towards us, we can still learn something from our interaction with them (e.g. how to deal with difficult people)! When you start to see the world as your classroom, you turn every single conversation you start into a very positive opportunity for self-growth!

I always see starting a conversation with a stranger as a win-win situation. It's a prize every time! If you find out you've got something in common or feel a real connection with the person, that's brilliant – you can seize this opportunity to forge a new friendship, expand your contacts book or maybe even pursue a new romance!

But even if it turns out this person does not want to talk or is just not your cup of tea, then that's not a problem at all! You can simply take this opportunity to practice your social skills and get better at handling difficult people! Just because you don't see eye-to-eye with somebody, that doesn't mean that they can't teach you something or that you can't enjoy a good conversation with them!

 One of the things that most people struggle with when it comes to starting conversation with a stranger is a fear of rejection.

But just think about it: if a stranger started a conversation with you, would you actually just stand there and be rude to their face? Would you actively reject their attempts at being friendly?

No, of course, you wouldn't...unless you are shockingly deficient in even the most basic of social skills! You would instead not only be polite and courteous, but you would also most probably be quite delighted that someone has made the effort to acknowledge your existence!

As we know, when someone takes an interest in us, it makes us feel so good about ourselves! And so when you are striking up conversation with a stranger, just remember that you are highly likely to end up making their day.

Unless they have the social skills of a snail, they are not going to reject or ridicule you for making small talk. Instead, **they are going to be absolutely delighted about the fact that you are taking such an active interest in their life!**

So what are you waiting for? Starting conversation with strangers is a win-win strategy for social success and fulfilment in life!

In order to give you a bit of inspiration with starting the small-talk, I have put together my 'faultess fivestep model for small talk success!' It explains how you start the conversation, keep the conversation going and bring the conversation to a smooth close!

Here's my faultless five-step model:

1.MAKE EYE CONTACT: Eye contact conveys confidence and sincerity. It is the essential first step for starting a conversation – you need to look at the person in order to send them a signal that you're looking to start a conversation with them! Eye contact is essential for conveying that you are completely confident and self-assured (even if you're feeling terrified inside) – and this is exactly what people need to see!

2.SMILE: Your smile is your secret weapon. Give someone your very best mega-wat smile and they will give you anything that you want! Studies have shown that smiling makes you instantly appear more attractive, likeable and approachable. Every small talk conversation must start with your biggest and best smile – let your beaming face be a beacon of confidence, positive energy and warmth! Give every single person you come across in life your very best smile – you will not only convey your own confidence but also signal that you are a likeable and approachable human being.

3.SAY HELLO: Worried about what to say? Don't be! Starting a conversation is literally as simple as saying HELLO. That is ALL IT IS – ONE SINGLE WORD! Clear your throat and say it clearly – as long as you sound confident, you will have no problem whatsoever in starting a fabulous conversation! You might add the classic British question 'how are you?' (without expecting an answer to that question!) or you might launch straight into your small talk leading statement. Whatever you choose to do, remember to deliver your first 'hello' with as much confidence and warmth as you can muster – this is guaranteed to lead to great small talk conversation!

4.USE A SMALL TALK LEADING STATEMENT: Now that you've made eye contact, given a big smile, and said hello, it's time to get down to business. But don't worry, it's really not that deep – small talk is all about keeping conversation non-controversial! Once you've said hello, it's time to use what I call a 'small talk leading statement'. This is where you use one of the following subject areas to make a light hearted and friendly remark: •**WEATHER:** My all-time favourite. Make a remark about the weather, for example 'isn't it hot today?' or 'I can't believe this weather, it's so cold!'

·THE LOCATION: Look around you and talk about where you are. For example, 'Isn't it lovely in here' or 'I never knew this place existed, I need to come here more often!'

·THE SEASON: This usually works best from September to December, when you can talk about how many shops are already selling Christmas cards and Christmas chocolate! Make a comment about the season, for example 'I can't believe it's Summer already' or 'I can't believe how quickly December comes around!'

·THEIR JOB: One of the number one small talk questions at any function is 'and what do you do?' – talking about someone's career usually keeps you on very safe territory (unless they're a CIA agent or just got fired). Ask whether they enjoy the job, what kind of hours they have to work, when they're next working, how they ended up in that career.

·LIGHT-HEARTED CURRENT AFFAIRS, for example the Royal Family: Make it your mission to catch up on the news every single day. This provides you with EXCELLENT small-talk conversation material! Keep informed on the news and you'll keep people engaged in conversation! Make sure you pick your topics wisely – make a remark about a TV show everyone's talking about, the latest Royal baby or wedding, or about a big story from the world of entertainment. You might talk about the fact Kylie Jenner isn't really a billionaire, how old Prince George is these days or that you can't believe Tom Jones is 80. Check the TV guide and see what big shows are on this week, because the chances are that someone you speak to today will be watching one of them! Check out the celebrity birthdays for that day so you are armed with some hot conversation topic to discuss over the water cooler!

5. BRING THE CONVERSATION TO A CONFIDENT CLOSE: Most people really struggle with ending a small-talk conversation. They don't want to appear rude or disinterested, and so don't have the heart to confidently bring the conversation to a close! The secret to successfully - and politely - ending a conversation is being both confident and courteous. Make an effort to excuse yourself - tell the person that you've got somewhere to be or something that you need to do. Make eye-contact, give them your very best smile, and tell them how lovely it has been to chat to them. Always remember to say 'have a good day!' and promise them that you'll catch up again soon. In order to end a conversation - and not be stuck talking to someone for hours on end - you need to get confident about bringing the discussion to a close. As long as you remain friendly and polite, you've got nothing to worry about! Remember to always leave people wanting more - make an exit and get on with your day whilst things are still going well and there is still more to say! That way, you'll have somewhere to pick up when you next see this individual!

A cheeky disclaimer to bring this five-step guide to a close: **always remember that when you're making small talk with a stranger, you should avoid bringing up politics, religion, sex and money!**

Making small talk with strangers should be seen as a bit of fun – don't feel anxious about it or feel scared of rejection.

See it as a little bit of excitement in your day…and also remember that one conversation could quite literally change your entire life!

You can never do too much networking and you can never make too many connections! See every stranger as a potential friend, business partner… or even fiancé!

Stop fearing rejection, stop feeling anxious about being judged and start making more conversation!

Small talk is a win-win situation, so stop worrying and start becoming the social star that you were born to be!

38. BEYOND BELIEF: FILLING THE RELIGIONLESS VOID

"To live is to suffer, to survive is to find some meaning in the suffering" - Nietzsche

'God is dead'. So declared the 19th century philosopher Nietzsche, heralding the arrival of an atheistic revolution across the Western world.

Today, the atheistic revolution is well and truly underway. The dawn of the 21st century saw the arrival of the so-called 'four horsemen of atheism' - Richard Dawkins, Christopher Hitchens, Sam Harris and Daniel Dennett - who injected new life and energy into the militant atheist movement.

'God', wrote Dawkins, 'is the most unpleasant character in all of fiction'. He has also described teaching your child to believe in God as a form of 'child abuse', before lamenting faith as 'the great cop-out, the great excuse to evade the need to think and evaluate evidence'.

Dawkins' comments perfectly capture the wider public mood and the most extraordinary sociological shift in religious belief and practice. In 2014, a YouGov poll found that over 77% of the UK population described themselves as 'not very religious' or 'not religious at all', with only 4% of the population identifying themselves as 'very religious'.

Religious belief is plummeting - science has become our new source of all knowledge and understanding, with Biblical myths about Creation and Salvation replaced with empirical proofs for a 'big bang' and evolution. Today, people no longer turn to the Bible in order to understand both themselves and the universe.

They instead worship at the altar of science, placing their faith in the test tube as opposed to the Cross.

What does this all of this mean for life as a human being in the 21st century? Whilst religion may no longer play such an influential and powerful role, **human beings still have the needs and desires that religious belief was once used to fulfil.** Whilst organised religion may have disappeared from our lives, **we still have those deep needs for meaning and spirituality in our lives.**

Dr Steven Reiss, a psychologist at Ohio State University, recently wrote about how the success of organised religion was due to its ability to fulfil 16 basic human desires.

These desires are:

- **Curiosity**

- **Acceptance**

- **Family**

- **Honour**

- **Idealism**

- **Independence**

- Order

- Physical Activity

- Power

- Romance

- Saving

- Social contact

- Status

- Tranquility

- Eating

- Vengeance

For hundreds of years, Christianity has fulfilled all of these basic human needs - and many more!

The Church has provided meaning, stability and purpose to people's lives, offering a pre-prepared framework for living a meaningful existence from cradle to grave.

The Church has served as the backdrop for meaningful moments in people's lives, such as their Baptism and Weddings, whilst the Ecumenical calendar is filled with reassuringly familiar annual events such as Christmas and Easter.

Through religious belief, millions of individuals have been able to find deep meaning and a real sense of morality in their otherwise uncertain and potentially overwhelming lives.

Yet many of the key teachings at the heart of organised religion have today been exposed as nothing but wish fulfilment and fiction. **People have abandoned organised religion and turned instead to science.** They no longer worship the crucified Jesus Christ or the creator God of Genesis, but instead worship science, individuality and the the cult of capitalism.

Here is the problem that we now face: God may be 'dead' and religious belief may now be abandoned, but our deep human desires for meaning, belonging, purpose and identity remain. **Each and every human being craves meaning and purpose in their lives.** We all want to know why we are here on this planet and we all want to live a truly fulfilling life.

If we do not find our meaning and purpose through prayer or religious worship, then where do we find our fulfilment as human beings?

I passionately believe that existentialism offers us the very best answer. Put simply, **existentialism is the philosophical belief that whilst life may have no inherent purpose** (as Bertrand Russell says, 'the universe is just there, and that's all), **every single human being has the potential to give their lives real purpose and meaning.**

Every single human being has the opportunity to create a very real purpose for their life. You are born without any purpose or meaning. In the same way that every other animal 'just exists' as part of the universal order, so do you! B**ut as a cognitively advanced and intelligent human being, you have the extraordinary ability to invent or discover a purpose for your life.** You can do this by transcending your basic needs and desires - for food, shelter and sex, for example - and **by committing yourself to a greater good or a greater cause**. You can **choose** to stop merely 'existing' as a Homo Sapien and instead thrive as a purpose-driven and deep-thinking human being!

For many years, religion provided a pre-packaged model for a meaningful and purpose-driven life. The Church would tell people that they had been lovingly created by God and that it was their purpose in life to follow God's commandments.

Today, there is nobody telling you what your purpose in life is - you must determine that purpose for yourself! You must, in other words, invent a meaning for your existence.

Many people decide to make money and fame the meaning of their lives - they believe that the purpose of human life is to make as much money as you possibly can! Others believe that the purpose of their human life is to simply 'get through it' as best they can, keeping their head down and desperately hoping to just survive each day.

I passionately believe that the purpose of your life is to AC-TIVELY CREATE a deep purpose for your life. Your purpose in life is to make your existence meaningful. You should strive to make your lifetime as fulfiling as possible!

You need to invent a meaning for your existence and strive to find genuine fulfilment, contentment and inner peace within your own very soul. **That means living a life inspired by your core values and with a deep commitment to fulfilling your potential as a human being.** Religion may no longer have the influence that it once had, but our deep need for a life of meaning, regulation and morality still remains.

In the 21st century, **you must take full responsibility for creating this purpose-driven life for yourself.** That means thinking existentially - *it is your duty to discover a real meaning and purpose for your existence!*

39. KNOWLEDGE
IS POWER

"Knowledge is the new rich...arm yourself with it!" -
Toni Payne

'Knowledge is power' wrote Thomas Jefferson, one of
the Founding Fathers and first-ever Presidents of the
United States. Jefferson proclaimed: **'Information is liberating....Education is the premise of progress, in every society,
in every family'.**

It is absolutely clear that the cultivation of knowledge is the
secret to achieving success in this world. The greatest source
of empowerment, and the best provider of opportunity available to human beings is the discipline that we call 'education'.

With education, absolutely anything is possible. Through
the cultivation of knowledge and the development of essential life skills, human beings are handed the power to completely revolutionise their whole entire lives.

**I believe very passionately in the concept of 'empowerment
through education'.** The gift of an education is the greatest
gift that anybody can ever give or receive. Receiving a good
education opens up an unlimited number of doors and oppor-

tunities. Education is the fastrack to success and the fundamental first element for living a genuinely happy and deeply fulfilling life.

The past 300 years have seen the most remarkable advances in the quality of human life. Life expectancy rates have soared whilst scandalous injustices such as slavery and imperialism have finally been consigned to the history books. Individual human beings have more rights and autonomy than ever before, and there is greater equality of opportunity today than there ever has been at any other point in human history. How has this positive transformation taken place? What has been the catalyst for this radical shift in the way human beings live their lives?

I believe the reason for this extraordinary revolution is the rapid increase in access to education around the world. In 1820, only 12% of the world population were able to read or write. Today, that statistic has been flipped on its head - in 2016, only 14% of the world population remains illiterate. That means over 86% of the global population is now able to read and write.. There is, I believe, a direct relationship between the improvement in people's quality of life and this improvement in access to good quality education.

That's because **when you educate a child, you completely and utterly transform their life**. You provide them with essential skills that will open up an unlimited number of doors and opportunities.

When you give a child the gift of an education, you give them the gift of a brighter future. **You enable them to escape their current conditions and give them the chance to make a real success of their life.**

Through education, our young people are taught how to think

for themselves, speak for themselves and make a living for themselves!

As a result, they are able to start living a successful, meaningful and fulfiling life! **Knowledge is power and education leads to empowerment! An education is therefore the greatest gift, opportunity, and blessing that anyone can ever receive!**

Education - which the vast majority of people in the Western world take for granted - is the most incredible source of individual empowerment. It is the reason our species is able to evolve, improve and progress, and it is the reason that people born into poverty and deprivation are able to totally transform their entire lives. Education empowers the most oppressed, impoverished, and stigmatised in our society. **The pen really is the most powerful weapon in our battle against inequality, injustice, and inhumane oppression of countless human beings. Knowledge really is power.** In the words of the incredible Malala Yousafzai, 'One child, one teacher, one book and one pen can change the world'.

As Yousafazi continues: **'With guns you can kill terrorists. With education you can kill terrorism'.** It is beyond doubt that education is the most powerful and effective weapon available in our fight against inequality, sexism, homophobia, racism, extremism, oppression...and every other kind of injustice!

Education transforms lives. Education empowers individuals by teaching them how to confidently accumulate knowledge and cultivate understanding. **It gives people an independence, a voice and a brighter future.** It equips individuals with the ability to think, evaluate, and critique for themselves.

When we receive an education, we can no longer be kept as slaves by oppressive systems of government, but we instead become the free-thinking and informed masters of our own destiny.

Education is the enemy of the world's dictators and oppressors. Knowledge gives the people the power that they so desperately deserve, and education gives everyday people the freedom to actually think for themselves.

If we want to change the world, we have got to make a commitment to giving every single young person a good education.

In my personal life, I know that **education and the pursuit of wisdom is our greatest source of salvation**. Through my reading of the daily newspapers and my study of history's finest works of philosophy, I have been able to totally transform my outlook on life and open the door to the most extraordinary opportunities.

My pursuit of education - primarily through the reading of current affairs and non-fiction books - has equipped me with an ability to think, write, speak, and articulate myself with real confidence and composure.

My understanding of current affairs and my fascination with complex philosophical questions has become a real 'secret weapon' for both academic and social success!

I am absolutely convinced that **we must all be active in pursuing education and working hard to accumulate more knowledge and understanding**. This knowledge and understanding should be about both ourselves and the world around us.

Knowledge really is power, and education really is the greatest source of human empowerment.

Whatever you do and wherever you go in life, always remain committed to the cultivation of knowledge and the never-ending engagement with education.

See the world as your classroom and see every person, experience, and opportunity as your next lesson.

Never tire of becoming more intelligent, informed, and innovative as you go through your life!

Becoming the best version of yourself begins with a commitment to becoming the most informed and educated individual that you possibly can be!

Knowledge is power - let's get empowered through education!

40. LET'S GET PHILOSOPHICAL!

"Education is the kindling of a flame not the filling of a vessel" (Socrates)

"The unexamined life is not worth living". So said Socrates, the founding father of Western philosophy.

According to Socrates, the only thing that we can ever know with certainty is the fact that we actually know nothing. He famously once remarked that **"I know that I am intelligent because I know that I know nothing"**.

Indeed, Socrates passionately believed that **"true knowledge exists in knowing that you know nothing"**.

The very first step on the journey towards living a philosophical and intelligent life is coming to the realisation that **what you know is a drop, and what you don't know is an ocean.**

As human beings in the 21st century, we are extraordinarily complacent about what we *think* we know about both ourselves and the world.

With so much information available at our finger tips – from the newspapers, history books and the internet – it's very easy to start believing that you know absolutely everything there is to know about every topic known to mankind.

As a result, we start to become overly-confident in our opinions and dangerously self-assured about the foundations of our worldly knowledge.

We become extremely complacent about our knowledge – we become so sure that our world view is the right one that we are unable to empathise with anyone else's. John Stuart Mill famously referred to this as the **'deep slumber of a decided opinion'.**

When we start to think that we already know all of the answers to life's biggest questions, we become lazy about attaining new knowledge and understanding. We become very closed-minded and get far too comfortable in our own world view.

The Western education system does nothing to help alleviate this 21st century problem. **Our schools see children as empty vessels that need to be filled with a certain amount of knowledge.**

The examination system used by our schools means that students spend their days in school being taught nothing other than how to answer exam papers.

 This gives them the false impression that there is a very clear limit to the amount of knowledge that they will ever need to attain. The message being projected is this: **as long as you know everything on the course syllabus, then you know everything that you could ever possibly need to know about this topic.**

Students are taught that the only purpose of learning is to pass an exam. *Instead of teaching young people how to think for themselves, the education system is focused solely on teaching them how to think in a way that will enable them to pass an exam.*

As a result, attaining knowledge through education becomes nothing more than a shallow and superficial means to an end.

This is a major problem, because education and learning do not just end on the day that you sit your last school exam. Students need to realise that learning is not just some 'means to an end' that will enable them to pass an exam or get a certain grade.

Attaining knowledge needs to be understood as a worthy end in itself!

Learning is for life, not just for your GCSEs or A Levels!

How much of the information that you were taught at school do you actually remember today? How much of the information that you were taught at school did you forget the very second that you finished your final exam?

The attainment of knowledge should be seen not as a means to an end (in order to pass an exam) but instead as a lifelong pursuit that is designed to help you to become the very best version of yourself!

Human beings are not empty vessels who need to be filled with a finite amount of knowledge.

There is no singular amount of knowledge that is universally agreed to be 'sufficient'. *The rapidly evolving pace of scientific research and intellectual breakthroughs means that what you learned in school 10 years ago will not still be factually correct in 10 years time!*

You therefore cannot afford to solely rely on the finite amount of knowledge that you picked up from your science textbook back in Year 10. Schools cannot just teach you 'what' to think but must instead teach you 'how' to think, learn and discover things for yourself.

We need to realise that **knowledge is not just a case of ticking the correct box on a multiple choice exam question!**

Instead, **the pursuit of knowledge must be seen as a worthy goal in itself.** We should not be learning at school just so that we can pass an exam – **we should be learning for the sake of our personal, social and moral development as a human being!**

Our schools should focus not on teaching young people *what* to think but focus instead on **teaching them *how* to think for themselves**!

Students need to stop memorising textbooks and start thinking, critiquing, analysing, and evaluating for themselves!

Education should be about discussion and evaluation, rather than recital and repetition.

If we travel back over 2,500 years to the days of Ancient Greece, we will find a truly extraordinary - and incredibly successful - approach to education.

At Plato's Academy and Aristotle's Lyceum, students were not being taught how to memorise a textbook or how to improve their exam techniques. Instead, these students were being couraged to engage in deep philosophical discussion and debate.

Education in Ancient Athens was all about the discussion of philosophical ideas and the cultivation of good character.

Children were to be trained in music, art, literature, science, maths and politics.

Students were not just conditioned to become exam-passing robots, but were instead encouraged to grow into intelligent, philosophical and autonomous human beings.

Rather than being robots in an exam factory, the youth of Ancient Greece were being taught how to flourish through life.

This is exactly what education should be all about – **schools should stop trying to become the best exam factory in the area and instead start aspiring to produce intelligent, inquisitive and autonomous human beings.**

Teachers should not just be preparing their students to pass an exam, but should be preparing them for life in the real world as well! Teachers should aspire to inspire their students to become confident young people with a desire to go out into the world and make a real diffference in society.

Schools should not be judged by their exam results but by the extent to which their alumni can successfully contribute to the common good of society.

As Socrates once remarked, **'Education is the kindling of a flame, not the filling of a vessel'.** Teachers should seek to to inspire a love for learning, rather than simply teaching students how to pass an exam. **Education should not be a factory farm but instead the facilitator of human flourishing.**

In the words of Aristotle, **'Educating the mind without educating the heart is no education at all'.** Our schools must aspire to cultivate well-rounded and free-thinking individuals who can go out into the world and truly thrive. Students are being failed by an education system that seeks to provide them with nothing more than the techniques needed to pass an exam. **Our young people are consequently entering adulthood without a clue how to think, critique or evaluate for themselves.**

Knowing how to get an A* on an exam paper does not help you to flourish and thrive in the real world!

Our schools need to take some real inspiration from the educators of Ancient Greece. Why do you think that Ancient Greece became the birthplace of Western philosophy and civilisation?

The reason for Ancient Greece's extraordinary success is very clear – it is all thanks to their education system!

That's right - **Ancient Greece was able to produce so many incredible thinkers and philosophers because its schools were focused on the cultivation of character and on the development of ideas.** The Athenian schools encouraged debate and discussion rather than endless hours of exam revision.

In order to emulate the extraordinary success of the Athenian educational enterprise, our young people must be encouraged to engage in vigorous philosophical discussion and open-minded political debate.

Education must be about the kindling of a lifelong flame, rather than the linear filling of a vessel. We must therefore encourage our young people to question more, evaluate more and strive to *become more* as human beings.

Our schools must be inspired by the wise words of Socrates, who said that '**To find yourself, [you must] think for yourself'.**

Our education system must not just teach young people what to think or what to know in order to pass an exam. Instead, our schools must strive to teach students how to think, debate, critique and evaluate for themselves!

Our time in school should be the very beginning of a lifelong pursuit of understanding and knowledge. **Teachers should** strive to plant seeds of knowledge and a love for learning that will grow forever.

Classrooms must therefore become safe spaces for debate, discussion, conversation and critique. **We desperately need to axe the exam factory approach and instead build an education system that produces well-rounded, self-aware and philosophically-minded human beings!**

This approach is already being pioneered by some of the nation's leading private schools, where students are taught social, oratory and debating skills as well as the content already found on the national curriculum.

State-school students, by contrast, are being left behind and are missing out on these essential life skills. If we want to aid social mobility and provide equal opportunity across the British Isles, we need to tackle this scandalous injustice immediately! Every single student at every single school in the UK - and indeed around the world - should taught not only the basics in english and maths, but also the basics in how to think, critique, discuss, articulate and evaluate with confidence.

Every single young person deserves a chance to learn social skills, debating techniques and as a result have the chance to get ahead in life!

We need to equip our young people with all of the resources needed in order to succeed in 21st century Britain.

We need to instil our young people with the confidence, emotional intelligence and resilience that will allow them to thrive through modern life!

With this in mind, here are a couple of concepts from the academic study of philosophy that would be brilliant additions to the school curriculum. *Headteachers take note!!*

By spending just one hour a week discussing these important topics, our schools could stop being such soul-destroying exam factories and start becoming innovative Schools of Life instead!

Let's take a look:

- **Epistemology** – The theory of knowledge. How do we attain knowledge? Are we born as a 'blank slate' (as 16th century philosopher John Locke believed) or is 'all learning remembering' (as Plato believed)? In the western world we use a system called 'empiricism' – we believe that all knowledge is attained through experience. Is there anything that we don't know through experience? For example, how do we know about morals? How is religious knowledge different to scientific knowledge? What evidence is sufficient in order for someone to believe that something is true?

- **Ethics** – How do we know the difference between right and wrong? What makes one behaviour moral and another behaviour immoral? Should we judge the morality of an act by the intrinsic good/bad of the act itself (an approach known as deontological ethics) or should we judge the morality of an act by its consequences (an approach known as teleological ethics)? Is morality universally agreeable or is 'the good' subjective to each individual and each culture? For example, are there any moral rules that are agreed by every single human being (e.g. that murder is wrong) and what moral rules are subjective to different societies (e.g. that homosexuality is wrong)? Where should get our moral guidance from – does religion have a role to play in our 21st century lives? Or should science seek to provide the answers to moral questions?

- **Metaphysics** – The question of existence. What does it mean to exist as a human being? How can we be sure that we even exist in the first place? What do we know with certainty about our own existence? How did the universe come into existence and what – if anything – does its existence depend on?

• **Political Science** – How should we govern a country? What political system is best – and why? What makes democracy the right form of government for the United Kingdom? What are the strengths and weaknesses of this political system, and how does it compare to other systems used around the world? How should we feel about alternative models of political government, for example the theocracy in many Middle Eastern countries or the socialist republic in China? How can we as individuals engage with our political system and how does our political system serve the needs of the people?

• **Aesthetics** – The discussion of beauty and artistic taste. What makes something art? How do we define and measure beauty? What does it mean for something / someone to be beautiful – is it all about appearances or is beauty more than skin deep?

Schools urgently need to shake off their fixation with 'filling the vessel' and start facilitating human flourishing instead!

Education is not about the relentless manufacture of outstanding exam results, but is instead about the nurturing of intelligent, autonomous and free-thinking young minds.

Our schools should stop being so obsessed with exam data and start focusing instead on the production of well-balanced young people.

Schools should get serious about producing intelligent and socially-conscious individuals who can go out into the world and make a positive contribution to the common good of society.

This all begins with ditching the recitation and revision, and focusing instead on the cultivation of character.

It's time to start getting philosophical in our schools...and to therefore start giving all of our young people a real chance to thrive through life!

41. NEVER GET BITTER, ALWAYS GET BETTER

'Ultimately, you are not defined by what has happened to you but by how you choose to respond' (Ben Wardle)

It's very easy to go through life with a real chip on your shoulder. There's something very addictive about taking on the victim mindset, and it's incredibly easy to start blaming everybody else for all the problems in your life.

Indeed, it's quite easy to spend your whole entire life blaming the world for the circumstances in which you find yourself. Sometimes, you might have a valid point.

But when you look at the bigger picture, you realise that there is little to be gained from constantly complaining about what other people - or what inanimate objects - have supposedly done to you.

When someone causes you harm, it is perfectly normal to feel hurt. This is especially true when it appears this harm was caused in a malicious and targeted way – no one likes to feel personally attacked and it is perfectly normal to be emotionally affected by this experience.

However, it is important to remember this: **in life, you are not** defined by what has happened to you but by how you have chosen to respond.

Allow me to explain: you have absolutely no control over how other people choose to treat you. You have no control whatsoever over the challenges that the universe sends you.

But what you do have absolutely full control over is how you choose to respond. And this is all you need!

That's right, we do not need any more power than the ability to choose how we respond.

The fundamental truth is this – **you are not defined by what has happened to you but by how you have chosen to respond**.

When someone causes us harm in any way, it is very slip into the 'victim mindset' where we dwell on what has happened to us and complain about how life isn't fair.

You are perfectly entitled to do this – after all, complaining or feeling sorry for yourself isn't a crime! But here's what you've got to ask yourself: **just how helpful is carrying this chip on your shoulder?**

What benefits will believing that you are a helpless victim actually bring to your life?

The truth is this: **When you allow yourself to become consumed by anger about how someone has treated you, you hand all power and control over your life and your happiness to that person!**

It is so easy to get bitter about things that have happened to us in the past. We all too willingly incarcerate ourselves in the prison of our past experiences, where we are unable to let go and move on with our lives.

Let's keep things real - the victim mentality does not benefit you in any way, shape, or form. It brings nothing but negativity, anger, and frustration into your life.

By taking on the victim mentality, we end up creating so much unnecessary suffering for ourselves.

When we see ourselves as a victim of the universe, we let unfortunate events of the past - which should never have been taken personally - totally destroy our happiness and inner peace in the present.

When we see ourselves as this victim, we become extremely bitter – we start to treat every single person we meet with deep suspicion and begin to see the entire universe as a very hostile and unfair place.

It is very clear that this mindset achieves absolutely nothing but the self-sabotage of our own happiness and success.

Choosing to be defined by our past in this way means that we can never make peace with the pain we are carrying around inside, and we forever walk around with a real chip on our shoulder.

But here's the good news - there is another way! Instead of becoming a bitter victim of our past, we can instead choose to become an empowered survivor.

Instead of being defined by what has happened to us, we can instead choose to grow what we go through!

Indeed, **we can choose to make peace with our past and take back control of our lives as autonomous human beings!**

This process of taking back control and becoming an empowered survivor all starts with that essential realisation that **you are not defined by what has happened to you but by how you have chosen to respond.**

Instead of becoming bitter because of the past, you can choose to get better instead. You can see what happened to you as an **opportunity for personal growth**.

You can turn that trauma into a learning opportunity and **make a conscious decision to rise above your experience.**

Instead of being defined by what happened to you, use it to become the best version of yourself.

Here's how I see it: You should thank the universe for bringing you every so-called 'blessing in disguise' – because of everything that has happened to you in your life, you have been able to grow into a stronger, wiser, and more resilient human being.

Because of what has happened in the past, you have been able to learn so much about rising above adversity and knowing your inner strength and worth!

Whilst we may not have deserved to go through the difficult challenges we have faced in the past, we don't deserve to be unhappy for the rest of our lives because of our past trials and tribulations!

Instead of being defined by what once happened to us, we deserve to take every trauma we have experienced and transform it into something life-enhancing!

Don't let your past experiences make you bitter or leave you feeling that you have been broken – **choose to use these life lessons from your past as opportunities to become a better human being!**

The people who have hurt you in the past do not deserve to have any power over your future. **Do not let what they did to you yesterday continue ruining your life tomorrow!**

You deserve freedom from the prison of your past!

You deserve to take back control and reclaim autonomy over your own life! I like to think of it like this - **'they were once my cup of tea, but I drink champagne now!'**

When it comes to reflecting on what has happened in our past, we always have a very clear choice. We can choose to let ourselves get bitter...or we can choose to become better as a person by using this experience as a catalyst force for change.

I hope that you will choose to transcend what has happened to you and use your past traumas as opportunities to blossom into a better, happier, and more resilient individual.

Remember - you can never be happy in life if you are always feeling bitter about what once happened to you.

As St Paul writes in his letter to the Galatians, 'the fruit of the spirit is love, joy, peace, forbearance, kindness, goodness, faithfulness, gentleness and self-control' (Galatians 2:22).

We need to fill our lives with these positive virtues - and that means choosing not to get bitter but to become a better person instead.

This means that instead of believing you are a victim of your past, you should strive to become someone who transcends past traumas and becomes a stronger individual because of them.

Don't keep choosing to be a wounded and powerless victim of your past.

Take back your control and choose to live your life as an empowered survivor.

42. MAKE PEACE WITH YOUR PAST

"The truth is, unless you let go, unless you forgive yourself, unless you forgive the situation, unless you realise that the situation is over, you cannot move forward" (Stephen Maraboli)

How many of us spend our lives wishing that we could change something about our past? How much time do we spend regretting decisions that we have made, opportunities that we have missed or regretting things that we have said? How frequently do we beat ourselves up for having not changed something about a situation we were in sooner or berate ourselves for not making more of an effort with someone whilst we had the chance?

It is only human to reflect on our lives so far and ask those 'what if...' questions. It is only human to look back on what we have experienced and wonder if we might have done things differently. There's nothing wrong with indulging in a bit of reflection on the past.

I think it is very true to say that we are all shaped by the experiences we have been through.

We can all take away important lessons from the mistakes

that we have made and from the experiences that we have been through. You know my mantra: **you grow through what you go through!**

We can choose to see our experiences from the past as opportunities sent by the universe to help us grow into stronger, wiser, and more confident human beings. Indeed, I believe that seeing our previous life experiences as positive 'life lessons' is a very healthy way of understanding our past.

Yet most people unfortunately do not have this healthy kind of relationship with their past. So many people instead have a very painful relationship with their memories of past regrets, mistakes and experiences. And a result, many people live life today as a prisoner to the pain of their past.

 In order to find happiness and fulfillment in our lives, we must take responsibility for liberating ourselves from the prison of our past experiences.

Your journey to freedom begins with the realisation of an absolutely essential truth: **the past is a place of reference not a place of residence.**

Let's explore this idea in a little more detail. I passionately believe that must learn to see the past as a fruitful source of life lessons, rather than as somewhere that we must remain permanently trapped. **The past is what you have been through, not who you are as a human being today**. We therefore need to make peace with the past – it's time to stop beating yourself up for mistakes that were once made. It's time to stop limiting your enjoyment of life today because of something you wish had done differently many years ago!

The only thing that we ever have any power over is our experience of the present and our plans for the future. We should therefore strive to invest all of our energy into learning from the past, rather than trying to change it. Here's what you need to know: **'The past cannot be changed, forgotten, edited or erased; it can only be accepted'**.

So, how do we actively go about making peace with our past? I believe that there are three essential steps: (1) acknowledging what happened, (2) accepting it as part of your history, and (3) allowing yourself to learn a lesson before moving on from it.

Let's explore these in more detail..

• **Acknowledge it** – we cannot be free from our past if we are denying it ever happened. We have to acknowledge what has happened in our past and validate the memories and feelings we are having. Suppression is not the solution to uncomfortable memories or feelings. We have to acknowledge them by making space for them and recognising them – you can handle these feelings and it is you who has the power over how they affect you going forwards into the future. You need to let yourself be vulnerable and let yourself acknowledge what actually happened before you will be able to move on.

• **Accept it** – This is the process of realising that the past cannot be erased or changed, it can only be accepted. We have to recognise that what has happened has happened – and that no amount of wishful thinking, anger or regret can do anything to change it. We must make peace with the fact that we cannot now change our past. In order to heal, we must give ourselves permission to be free from the prison of the past. When we find the strength to accept that we can't change what has happened, the past is no longer able to wield power over us. Acceptance is about making peace with your past – you come to terms with what you have been through and you give validation to your feelings about it. You embark on a journey towards letting your desperation to change the past go. The first essential step on this journey is realising that all we can transform now is our present moment and the future. Once we have acceptance, we can look back on that event as part of our story, without being overwhelmed by it.

• **Allow yourself to learn a lesson and let go** – This is the most important part of the healing process. It is absolutely essential that you are able to learn a lesson from the experience that will help you as you move forward into the future. This way, you don't try and suppress what has happened but instead use that experience in a positive and life-affirming way. You can choose to grow from what happened and rise above any pain and suffering that experience once produced. You might even be able to use your experience to help others and turn tragedy from the past into triumph. When we share our story, we start important conversations that have the power to completely transform people's lives! In order to heal, we must make peace with the fact that whilst we can never change what happened to us, we can choose to learn from our experience. We can choose to rise above the pain of our past and grow into positive, inspiring and fulfilled human beings.

I want to conclude this chapter with the words of Edith Eger, the inspirational Holocaust survivor who has brought hope and healing to millions of people around the world. She is a personal hero and inspiration of mine, and I strongly urge you to read her extraordinary book 'The Choice'.

In this book, in which Eger recounts her experiences as a young girl being held in Auschwitz Concentration Camp, Eger guides the reader through her journey to understanding what had happened to her and finding hope for the future. On arrival at Auschwitz, Eger had been with both her mother and sister.

That was the last day Eger would ever see her mother – she had watched as her mother had been sent off to the gas chambers after being deemed not fit enough to be used for gruelling slave labour at the camp.

She writes: **"Here you are! In the sacred present. I can't heal you – or anyone – but I can celebrate your choice to dismantle the prison in your mind, brick by brick. You can't change what happened, you can't change what you did or what was done to you. But you can choose how you live now. My precious, you can choose to be free".**

We must realise that we can't change the past, but that we can choose how we live now.

We can choose to be free and make peace with our past!

Remember that you deserve nothing less than complete happiness in your life today!

The journey to genuine happiness begins with deciding to let go of the pain of your past.

And so I wholeheartedly pray that you will make that choice today!

Be free from the pain of your past - and allow yourself to thrive into the future!

43. LET GO OF GRUDGES

"Forgive others, not because they deserve forgiveness but because you deserve peace" (Jonathan Lockwood Huie)

Jesus famously said that you should 'forgive not seven but seventy-seven times'. He believed very strongly that you should never tire of forgiving and must be selfless in showing those who have treated you badly compassion.

This all sounds very saintly and, of course, it is...we are talking about the teachings of Jesus Christ afterall! But here's the thing: practicing forgiveness may indeed be selfless, but is also extremely self-rewarding as well! **That's because you gain a lot of reward for *yourself* when you start making forgiveness your new priority in life**!

Allow me to explain. Many people assume that forgiveness is a sign of weakness that achieves nothing other than to make you look extremely foolish. This is absolutely wrong! **As Jesus beautifully illustrated over 2,000 years ago, forgiveness is actually a supreme act of confidence, strength and empowerment!**

That is because forgiveness is not about letting people off the hook but is instead about taking back your power and restoring inner peace in your own life!

Let me be very honest with you: one of my most problematic character traits is my inability to let go of grudges.

Apparently, this is common amongst Scorpios, so at least we know I can blame this on my star sign! Whenever I feel that someone has intentionally caused me harm – especially if they have tried to humiliate or manipulate me – I never fail to become absolutely incandescent with rage.

My best friends are regularly subjected to my rants about what people have done to me, with these rants always starting with the same three words "How DARE they…!!!'

I would always try and justify holding grudges like this: this person, I would say, has intentionally attempted to cause me harm, and so they are a nasty piece of work. They cannot be trusted and they deserve to pay a price for what they have done to me!

In my angry and defensive mind, I believe that I **have** to hold a grudge against them in order to make sure that they realise what they have done is wrong, and consequently then realise themselves what an awful person they are!

In reality, of course, this is just not how it works. **All that holding a grude ever achieves is the creation of more anger, frustration and victimisation in your own life.**

Whilst you wallow in your anger and frustration, the person who caused you so much harm gets on with their life as if nothing had ever happened.

Seeing the perpetrators lack of remorse leads to you feeling even more resentment and frustration, which then causes even more pain and suffering in your own life.

As you wallow in your victim status, they get on with living their life. And so not only have you let them hurt you in the past, but you are then allowing them to carry on hurting you into the future!

You are essentially signing yourself up to a lifetime of suffering and This has got to stop!

We have to realise that holding grudges hurts nobody but ourselves! Holding grudges is a clear sign that we have become far too sensitive and insecure for our own good.

Holding a grudge is, ultimately, a sign of weakness.

All that it does is show you up as a wounded, bitter and angry individual.

Your inability to move on demonstrates your lack of self-love and leaves you held hostage to a real victim mentality.

Being able to forgive others for what they have done to us is an absolutely essential life skill.

As Jesus teaches in the New Testament: **"You have heard it was said 'Love your neighbour and hate your enemy'. But I tell you, love your enemies and pray for those who persecute you, that you may be children of your father in heaven. He causes his son to rise on the evil and good, and sends rain on the righteous and the unrighteous' (Matthew 7:43).**

I always think of it like this - If you were secure, confident and happy in your own skin right now, surely you would not be so bitter about what has happened to you in the past? If you weren't so defensive and fragile about your public appearance and ego, surely you wouldn't be so scorned about the way somebody once behaved or made you feel?

A truly secure and confident person would acknowledge that

they had been hurt but would also realise that they deserve freedom from pain of the past.

A truly secure and confident person would realise that they deserve to heal, make peace with the past, and move on.

I therefore passionately believe that you should always strive to **forgive the situation, but not forget what the individual did.**

Most importantly, you should forgive the situation regardless of whether the individual involved either want forgiveness or even deserves to be forgiven.

The point is this: they might not deserve forgiveness, but you deserve peace. You deserve to let go of that anger and resentment. You deserve more happiness and contentment in your life!

I've realised that holding grudges hurts nobody but YOU. **Grudges are not only pointless, but they are also enduring sources of personal pain.**

You need to ask yourself whether that is really what you deserve in your life!

Here is what you need to do in order to let go of those grudges that you can't quite seem to shake off:

1. Acknowledge the harm that someone caused you. You need to realise that it is not weak to become aware of it. Stop being so defensive and let down your guard. Acknowledge exactly what somebody did to you and acknowledge exactly how they made you feel. Be vulnerable for a minute - identify exactly how this person hurt you and recognise how they made you feel. Give validity to your feelings – recognise them and accept them as yours. Realise that you are not defined by what someone else did to you – you are defined by how you choose to respond. Realise that what happened says more about the perpetrator than it says about you. Be confident that you will not be defined by what happened to you. Know that you can grow in resilience and strength as a result of this experience.

2. Picture the person you're holding a grude against in your mind. Acknowledge how you feel towards this person. How do you feel when you picture them in your mind? What effect does seeing them have on your whole body? Is there anything you find yourself wanting to say to them? Acknowledge how you feel. Now, try and actually feel sorry for them - the fact that they have attempted to cause you harm means that they cannot be happy themselves! Indeed, they must be driven by a lot of unhappiness and bitterness if they are causing harm to other people. Be thankful for the fact that you have now seen their true colours. You have seen what they are capable of. Thank the universe for showing you what they're really like – you will not be letting yourself get hurt by them again anytime soon! There will be no more falling for their lies, deceit, manipulation or other toxic behaviour! Now make a conscious effort to 'wish them well'. Say it to them, actively project it onto them. Know in your mind that they have no longer got any power over you whatsoever, and know with confidence that you are now stronger and more secure than they ever will be.

3. Forgive the situation and make peace with what happened to you. – Genuinely make peace with what happened and realise that it cannot be undone. Fully accept and forgive the situation - don't struggling against reality! By doing this, you are able to completely take back control. You are able to release yourself from the power that past actions continue to have over you. You are finally allowing yourself to be happy once again! Tell yourself that 'you can handle this with resilience and strength'. Know in your mind that you have the resilience and strength to make peace with the past, let go of your anger and confidently move forwards with your life. Be empowered in the knowledge that you have taken back control of the situation and have successfully made peace with your past. You are no longer going to be defined by what someone once did to you . Instead, you will now live life on your own terms and in accordance with your own values.

4. Allow yourself to move forwards in your life. Recognise that the power this negative person once had over you have gone. You are no longer a victim of the past but an empowered survivor who can finally move forwards in life. What happened is in the past and has no power over your present or your future. You will not be defined by someone else's negativity but by how you now consciously choose to live a life of positivity. People who hurt you in the past can no longer hurt you or rule over your mood in the present and in the future. The power is well and truly back in your hands! Wish the people who have hurt you in the past well, and free yourself from their grips. Take back your power as an empowered survivor - you are now the master of your own destiny! You will no longer be defined by the past!

Remember, people can only have power over you if you choose to give it to them. When we choose to hold a grudge, we choose to become a prisoner to our past. And when we choose to let go of our past, we choose to become an empowered survivor who is able to take back control of our life.

To forgive someone is not a sign of weakness but a liberating act of personal empowerment. It shows that you know your worth and it demonstrates your infinite resilience as a human being.

By practicing forgiveness, you are telling the world that you will not be a victim anymore!

Forgiveness is all about taking back control, finding empowerment from within and making peace with the past.

This process of 'letting go' means wishing the person well and choosing not to be defined by what they did to you but instead by how you have chosen to respond.

It is about choosing not to let yourself get bitter but instead deciding to get better.

Remember: you are not a passive victim of your past.

Instead, you are an empowered survivor who is taking back control of their life and becoming the author of their own future.

44. TURN IMPULSIVE REACTIONS INTO INTELLIGENT RESPONSES

"Between stimulus and response, there is a space. In that space is our power to choose our response. In our response lies our growth and our freedom" (Viktor Frankl)

Are you a slave to your impulses or the master of your own destiny? Do you live your life at the mercy of your emotions or you do make it your mission to intelligently manage them?

As conscious and rational human beings, we have a lot more control over our lives than we tend to realise.

Here's what I believe: **far too many people sleepwalk through life as slaves to their emotions, fears and desires. They fail to realise that they actually have the opportunity to take ownership of their life and become the master of their own destiny**.

The feeling of anger is a very good example of how people can easily become overwhelmed by extreme emotions. Feelings of anger can easily trigger impulsive emotional outbursts that we later bitterly regret.

In the 'heat of the moment,' we can say things or do things that we later deeply regret. We look back and don't recognise ourselves – it is almost like we became possessed and lost all control over our bodies and minds! Instead of living as a victim of impulsive reactions such as these, we can start consciously choosing to make intelligent responses.

We do not have to continue being controlled by our fears, desires and emotions.

We can choose instead to start acknowledging and accepting our feelings before choosing how we will intelligently respond to them!

The Holocaust survivor Viktor Frankl wrote that between stimulus [the trigger] and response, 'there is a space'. Within this mental space, we find **'our power to choose our response'**.

Realising that we possess this power is extraordinarily important – **it is your opportunity to become the master of your destiny.**

Realising this power is your opportunity to decide that you will not get bitter but get better.

It is your opportunity to express your emotions in constructive – as opposed to destructive – ways.

This opportunity is made available to every single one of us at every single moment in our lives.

No matter what the circumstances or how you feel, you always have the choice whether to impulsively react or intelligently respond.

No matter how strongly you feel, you always have control

over how you express your emotions. *You always have a choice between impulsively reacting or intelligently responding.*

It is completely our choice whether to express our feelings in constructive or destructive ways.

Will you choose to have a calm conversation about how you feel or will you just lash out in an angry fit of rage? Will you allow yourself to cry and break down, or will you unwisely attempt to bottle your sadness up?

Will you acknowledge your fears before working to make peace with them, or will you allow them to totally paralyse you and ruin your life?

Remember that your feelings are always valid. Your emotions must always be accepted.

But also remember that you do not have to just impulsively react to them in destructive ways!

Instead, you can choose – in that gap between stimulus and response – **to take a much more rational and mindful approach.**

You do not have to be a victim to your impulsive reactions. You instead have the power to choose an emotionally intelligent response.

This is a response that will allow you to confidently express your emotions and clearly communicate how you feel.

The choice is completely and utterly yours.

It is completely within your capabilities to turn impulsive reactions into intelligent responses.

Remember, this does not mean denying your emotions or trying to stage-manage your responses. Suppression only ever leads to depression!

Realise that there is a gap between 'stimulus' and 'response'.

This gap is golden, because it allows you to intelligently choose how you will respond.

Capitalise on this power to choose by cultivating emotional intelligence and start turning your impulsive reactions into intelligent responses.

45. HOW TO HANDLE THE HATERS

"Haters only hate things they can't have and the people they can't be. It's just a little thing called jealousy" (Lil Wayne)

When I first started posting on TikTok, I was shocked at the nasty things people would keep commenting on my videos. Whilst 99.9% of the comments would be overwhelmingly positive, there was still a very small minority of people who would comment things like 'I wish it would go kill itself' or 'this creature deserves to be put down...this is the reason I would never let my son be gay'.

Despite all the wonderfully kind and positive comments, it was always the horrible and hateful ones that would catch my attention and get stuck in my mind. At first, I was deeply hurt – how could someone say that about me? Did they not realise I that I was just a human being like them? How would they feel if someone spoke about them or their loved ones in that way?

My feelings of hurt very quickly turned into feelings of anger. I'd sit there reading these comments and be thinking how DARE they say these things to me! How DARE they be so rude, horrible, and cruel from behind their keyboard!

These comments started bringing back all the feelings associated with being judged and labelled when I was a kid. And I instantly felt my defensive mindset kicking in once again!

The more I read these hateful comments - which I don't advise that you ever do, by the way - the more incandescent with rage I became!

I was SO incensed – how dare these people have the nerve to tell me to kill myself or tell me that I was 'disgusting'! How dare they attack me and say these horrible things about me, simply for posting a video of myself ranting about the weather or harmlessly reacting to an Instagram filter!

When I had first started reading these nasty comments, I was completely and utterly overwhelmed by them. I genuinely believed that these internet trolls were saying what everybody else was secretly thinking.

As a result, I slipped back into that toxic mindset of believing I had to apologise for my 'too much' personality to every single person that I met.

I again started assuming that every single person I met would find me "too much" or "too gay". I always expected people to roll their eyes and make a passive-aggressive remark about my personality. I'd start conversations with comments like "I know I'm too full on and too much most of the time..." or "I promise I am intelligent and that I am a good person"!

I felt like I had to explain myself to everyone and to keep constantly apologising for my personality. It was like I had to keep putting myself down before anybody else had the chance to.

Looking back now, I can see that this was - of course - completely and utterly wrong. As I wrote back in part one of this book, you should never apologise for being who you authentically are.

Here is what you need to know: **anybody trying to put you down is already beneath you**. As I always say, the only thing you should ever apologise for in life is causing harm.

Remember John Stuart Mill's 'Non-Harm Principle'?! Here is what I started to think - **How is me being a little bit flamboyant and walking with a little bit of sass something to apologise for?** Why on earth am I apologising for my positive and friendly personality which has lifted the mood and kept everybody entertained? How dare you say I am 'too much' for you...who's to say that you're not the one bringing 'too little' to the table?!

As time went on, it started to dawn on me that if these anonymous trolls were being so cruel to me, then they were surely being just as cruel to thousands of other people on this app.

I was well aware that although I was only 20, I was still one of the older people using TikTok - and I became deeply concerned about how young people posting on TikTok would feel if received this kind of abuse.

What if, I worried, someone received one of these hateful comments on a video they had posted and then never used the app again? What if they completely took these hateful and vile comments to heart?

I realised that whilst I was now in such a confident and empowered place in my own life, so many people are not quite as able to shake off such horrible comments quite so easily. I know with certainity that if I had received this hateful kind of comment even just a couple of years ago, I would have been absolutely unable to cope.

If I'd been subjected to these anonymous online attacks when I was going through one of my insecure and sensitive phases, I would have undoubtedly taken every single word written about me to heart. This could have had catastrophic consequences for my self-esteem and mental wellbeing.

As you know, it is my personal motto to 'aspire to inspire'. And so I knew that I needed to do something to help other people suffering from this kind of online trolling and abuse.

Well aware that my I had 300K followers and an average of 15 million views a month, I knew that I wanted to use my platform as a force for good.

I wanted to send a very clear message to the people who followed me on social media that they did not have to be defeated or broken down by the nasty and horrible comments anonymous trolls were leaving on people's videos!

I wanted to show my followers that no matter what anybody says about you, it is your duty to continue being fearlessly authentic!

And so I made a promise to myself: **I will stand up for myself! I will be fearlessly authentic and absolutely certain of my worth as a human being! I was not going to let these nasty, stupid and rude litle people get me down!**

As you know, I strongly believe that **whilst everybody has the right to an opinion, nobody has the right to be hateful or cruel. <u>There is a very clear line between free speech and hate speech.</u>**

If these trolls thought they were going to get away with targeting me with hate speech, then they had got another thing coming! I more I thought about this trolling, the more I realised that anyone 'hating' on me was actually just very jealous of me.

They were evidently intimidated by my confidence and my ability to be unashamedly authentic on social media. They couldn't handle the fact that someone who was not conforming to their narrow-minded gender stereotypes could be so loud, confident and proud of who they were!

Perhaps, I thought, they were bullied for not conforming to stereotypes at school so they now lived a life of repression and couldn't stand to see someone actually being themselves.

If someone feels the need to attack you for your personality or appearance then you clearly triggering them in some way.

When someone attacks you, it says more about them than it could ever say about you. In fact, I think this: you should actually feel flattered to be the target of someone's attack – they clearly want what you've got, and they're angry that they're never going to get it!

Let's be very clear - **trolling must not be tolerated under ANY circumstances! It can never be justified and it should never before normalised.**

To be frank with you, I do not care what someone who is trolling might be going through in their lives. I do not give a TOSS if they are struggling to accept their sexuality or have been bullied by others in the past! There is never any excuse for intentionally causing harm to another human being!

The most important thing that to know about trolling is this - **you should never take it personally**. It is never a personal attack on you but is instead the expression of someone else's insecurity.

Hateful comments deserve absolutely none of your precious time and attention!

Remember, never listen to the opinion of someone you wouldn't take advice from. Would you ever take advice from a sad, lonely and pathetic anonymous troll?

Do you really aspire to be living the desperate, tragic and hate-filled existence that they are living? No, you do not!

Of course, you are allowed to be upset about what someone has said about you.

But what you are not allowed to do is take what some nasty online troll has said to heart!

Don't you dare even consider the idea that they might be right, and **don't you dare even <u>consider</u> apologising for being who you are because of the comments sad and pathetic trolls have made!**

I think everyone that with a social media platform has a different approach to dealing with trolls, in the same way that everyone has a different approach to dealing with any nasty comments or discrimination that they might face in everyday life.

And so you need to find the response strategy that works best for YOU. It needs to be a strategy that keep you safe - both physically and psychologically - and that makes you feel secure.

With that in mind, I want to share a few pieces of advice from my own 'response strategy' to online trolling.

As I say, it is my mission to 'aspire to inspire', and I regularly do so by taking the trolls down with humour and sass. Let me be clear - I am well aware that you can never stop people from trolling and that you will never 'win' in a battle against a troll.

But I do believe that you should never ever let yourself become a victim to trolling - **in life, you only get what you put up with. Never put up with someone else trying to put you down!**

❖ ❖ ❖

With this in mind, I hope you might find one or two pieces of the advice here helpful:

<u>**Do NOT take it personally.**</u> This point goes without saying. Do not take any trolling, negativity or rude comments personally. They are 100% about the person behind the keyboard and say 0% about you as a person. Trolling is someone projecting their insecurities and jealousy onto someone else – it is an expression of self-hatred and a shameless exercise in attention seeking. Really, you should feel sorry for the trolls! Do not take what they say to heart – you are absolutely perfect, whole and fabulous exactly as you are. You must be relentlessly authentic and know that you are a role model to the rest of the world in showcasing what it means to be a confident and authentic human being.

<u>**Do not get addicted to reading it.**</u> It is too easy to get addicted to reading people's negative comments about you. No matter how much you have this desire to find out what they're all saying, DON'T DO IT! It is an act of self-sabotage and will achieve nothing but lower your mood and leave you feeling angry and attacked. Remember that the trolls do not speak for the world but only their sad, lonely and insecure selves. Remember that your time is precious and that you don't have time to be reading these pathetic so-called 'opinions'. What other people think of you is none of your business – especially when they don't really think it but are just saying it for attention!

<u>**You can choose the 'report, block & ignore' approach.**</u> You

can choose to completely ignore what someone says – but you can also choose to respond and, as I like to say, put them back in their little boxes! Most people do choose to just completely ignore: 'report them, block them but whatever you do don't engage with them!' The idea behind this is that trolls are simply bored and lonely attention-seeking keyboard warriors who feed off getting a reaction out of people online. If you take the bait and bite back, you're giving them exactly what they want! Don't give them the satisfaction of a response – as Michelle Obama says, 'when they go low, we go high'.

You can choose the 'kill them with comedy' approach. If you feeling strong enough, take my very own 'kill them with comedy' approach. This is where you can turn people's negative you find a cure pal" on a recent video, I replied to his comment with a video stating "Yes dear, you're right - I hope we find a cure for your stupidity and ignorance soon! Go and find a brain cell my love…good luck because you'll need it". My response video gained me 140K views, thousands of likes, and hundreds of comments within hours – not to mention thousands of new followers on both TikTok and Instagram! I had totally shut down this rude and pathetic comment, entertained thousands of viewers and sent a very clear message to people watching about LGBT+ rights all in one go. If you're going to post rude comments on my content, I'm going to turn them to my advantage by using them to entertain and educate as many people as I can! If you can take any rude comment someone makes about you and turn it into a joke, you instantly disarm and undermine them.

Humour is a very powerful weapon in undermining bullies, trolls, and haters in that it allows you to take full control of the situation.

Never engage in conversation with a troll. Whilst you can bite back with a humorous punchline to any comment left on your public profiles, make sure you always leave it at that.

Never, ever under ANY circumstances engage in any kind of conversation with an internet troll. If they message you on private messaging, they must be blocked instantly. They do not deserve your dialogue and they do not deserve any kind of discussion. One humorous or sassy reply is fine and may be funny – but replying to any replies after that is a NO GO ZONE! It's all about taking control of the situation – the second you start entertaining conversation, you are handing power back to the trolls. They do not deserve one second of dialogue with you – you can publicly shame them but do not otherwise entertain them.

Always choose the 'don't get bitter, get better' approach. Whatever you do in response to trolling or hate, make sure it is not about getting bitter but getting better. I thank the trolls for their negative comments because it gives me a chance to make a put them down with a sassy one line response! It's nice to get that sass out of my system once in a while!

Never let the toxic and pathetic comments of online trolls lower your vibration as a human being – remember we are on a journey to becoming the best versions of ourselves. That means rising above it, perhaps making a joke out of it and being even more emboldened and confident in ourselves because of it. Don't you dare get bitter and join the trolls in their cesspit of negativity – you owe it to yourself to keep growing and keep glowing through life!

At the end of the day, haters deserve absolutely nothing from you. If you can use their nasty comments to your advantage, then go for it! **But make sure that you don't give the haters themselves any air time and attention whatsoever!**

Trust me when I say that **they are absolutely not worth it...do not feed them!** Instead, leave them to their negativity and focus on unashamedly being your fabulous self.

Indeed, I believe that you should **make it your mission to keep getting on their nerves!**

As far as I'm concerned, if I'm not getting on homophobic people's nerves, then I need to up my game!

Nothing gives me greater satisfaction than being unashamedly authentic and putting rude, ignorant and horrible little haters back in their box!

I aspire to inspire the people that I meet to live their most unashamedly authentic and deeply fulfilling life. I am therefore not going to let negative and irrelevant people who try to drag me down get in the way of my life's purpose!

The best way to silence the trolls is to keep being yourself no matter what hate they try and throw at you.

At all times, remember that you are so much better than them.

<u>Keep doing what you're doing and never lower yourself to their level.</u>

Just remember that there's a reason you're reaching new heights whilst they're wallowing in their own self-hatred and toxicity!

<u>You've got this - keep going and keep glowing!</u>

46. USE SOCIAL MEDIA RESPONSIBLY

"Like all technology, social media is neutral but is best put to work in the service of building a better world" (Simon Mainwaring)

Did you know that over 45% of the world's population now use social media, with the average person spending 2 hours and 23 minutes of their day on social media websites?

Social media has become the biggest sensation of the 21st century (*so far*). It has completely revolutionised the way in which we communicate, consume news ,and access information. It has totally transformed modern life and has connected people across the globe in ways that would have been completely unimaginable even 30 years ago.

Social media undoubtedly has countless benefits. It has most certainly made the world a better place. People are now more connected and informed than ever before. Anybody can become anybody thanks to social media - we can all share our thoughts at the touch of a button and we can all market ourselves to the world via the Facebook news feed.

As a result, traditional barriers to success have been abolished

- you no longer need to be of a certain class or to have attended a certain school in order to make it big. Anybody can become famous and anybody can get involved in whatever causes and campaigns matter to them.

My own life has certainly been transformed - in the most positive ways imaginable - by social media. Social media has opened countless doors and presented me with countless opportunities. **I would not be where I am or who I am today without social media.**

I have been able to post my revision videos on YouTube, share my blog posts on international news websites, and of course build up a following on the TikTok video sharing app! All of these self-publishing platforms have opened up big, life-changing opportunities for me - without them, I wouldn't have had 0.1% of the exposure I have been so fortunate to so far receive! Social media is a success because it gives the individual an opportunity to self-publish their content and become the author of their own success. Instead of depending on your family being well-connected to the entertainment industry or depending on attending a good school, anybody who lives anywhere has a 100% equal opportunity to 'make it big' on social media.

The internet is also the greatest educational resource that any of us could ever dream of accessing. When you go online, you have quite literally the entire world at your fingertips.

There are billions of articles, research papers and explanatory videos on literally every single topic under the sun. The internet is the biggest library in the universe - it is home to absolutely everything you could ever need to know about every single topic known to mankind.

I certainly put my academic success and my extensive knowledge about philosophy, psychology, mental health, human rights and world affairs down to my access to the internet. My extensive knowledge has not come from archaic text-books gathering dust in the local library - everything I know is thanks to the resources all available at our fingertips online!

It is very clear that social media and the internet have had the most extraordinarily positive impact on our world. The internet has empowered, educated and informed individuals like never before - everyone now has a voice and everyone now has access to both opportunities and also to information. The internet is the greatest human revolution! However, it is essential that we make a real effort to use the internet in a very responsible way. Because whilst the online sphere is so positive and beneficial, the internet can very easily become a source of immeasurable amounts of suffering and pain.

We're all very familiar with the dark side of social media - the body image pressures, trolling. bullying and, of course, the fake news and misinformation crisis.

Then there are the problems caused by the explosion in hard-core online pornography, which has made the most shock-ingly violent and extreme sexual content accessible at the click of a button.

I think the biggest problem that we are facing with social media is the blurred lines and boundaries between what people see online and what is actually going on in real life.

On Instagram, for example, we are bombarded with artifi-cially enhanced and heavily filtered images that do not per-petuate totally irrational and unrealistic expectations for personal appearance and body image. Waistlines are edited to look smaller and faces are airbrushed to look flawless - social media is extraordinarily superficial and nothing more than a fictional fantasy.

Almost everything on social media is fake - people buy fake followers, spread fake news, fake their appearances and boast about having fake online friends!

Over on Twitter, we are bombarded with misinformation and blatant lies masquerading as genuine 'news' stories.

'Fake news' is everywhere - on social media, the rules of truth, accuracy and transparency do not apply. As long as you present yourself in a confident and convincing way, you can get people to believe absolutely anything that you say!

Social media mobs regularly take matters in their own hands, 'cancelling' celebrities who put one foot wrong and assassinating the character of anyone not strictly conforming to their 'woke' activist agenda.

From behind an anonymous computer screen, so-called 'trolls' get away with saying whatever they want to whoever they want - receiving death threats and hate messages is just part of daily life for the vast majority of high-profile social media users.

Almost half of young people say they have been 'harassed' on the social media website Instagram, whilst at least one in three 12 - 17 year olds have been cyber-bullied online. At least half of all LGBT+ students have told researchers that they have been subjected to online harassment.

Over 83% of young people believe that social media companies should be doing more to tackle cyber bullying online.

Social media is a very artificial and angry place. It is extremely fake, in terms of both the images that people share of themselves and also in terms of the so-called 'news articles' that go viral. Social media is not - in any way, shape or form - an accurate reflection of the real world.

However, I do not believe it is a 'negative' space. **Instead, social media itself is a very neutral place - it is completely down to you how you choose to use, and how much you choose to engage with, the platform.**

If you go online and follow 100 motivational quotes accounts, for example, your experience of the internet is going to be very positive indeed! If you go online and follow 100 accounts promoting diet pills and sharing photoshopped bikini pictures, then you're experience of the online world is going to be totally different!

In the same way that I believe you must become the master of your destiny in the real world, it is absolutely essential that you take full responsibility for everything that you do in the online world.

You must take back control of your use of the internet and social media! You must be a rational and responsible user - do not let yourself get sucked in and become totally consumed by a fake and artificial online world!

It is essential that you use social media to your advantage and view the internet as a tool you can use in order to live a better life. You should not - under any circumstances - start making social media itself your whole entire life! **Social media is here to enhance your quality of life, not to take over your whole life!**

Use the internet's resources as a positive catalyst for growth and development. Use social media as a stepping stone towards success - it is a chance to put yourself out there and be proactive in making important connections.

But always see social media for what it really is! And always know what social media isn't - remember that social media is never an alternative to living in the real world!

Always prioritise your real life and your real relationships over your superficial social media status!

Make it your mission to only use social media as a means to an end - it should help you to live your best life, take over your life!

This means setting yourself clear rules and expectations for how you will use online platforms - know when it is time to put down your smartphone and stop letting notifications interrupt every single second of your day!

Be mindful about what accounts you follow and what sources of information you expose yourself to - you need to self-regulate your use of social media and ensure that it is used responsibly!

Most importantly, **Stop comparing your 'behind the scenes' to someone eles's highlight reel!**

Stop believing the fake news and stop buying into the fake body image myths being perpetuated by so-called 'influencers'.

Get serious about using social media in a responsible way - protect your mental health and stop living entire life through your smartphone.

Strive to keep it real and to keep putting your mental health first!

47. DON'T FEAR DIFFICULT CONVERSATIONS

"Be brave enough to start a conversation that matters… talking changes lives" (Ben Wardle)

People always say that you should never discuss religion, politics, or money. Add to that list sex, sadness and death, and I think that we've established a comprehensive collection of the discussion topics that people in our supposedly liberal society avoid like the plague!

People are terrified of talking about anything to do with dying, democracy, or depression. We avoid these tough topics like the plague – we do whatever we can to keep the conversation on the safe topics such as the weather or last night's TV! This small-talk is very helpful in social situations where we are chatting to people we hardly know. **But when it comes to starting conversations with our nearest and dearest, we should not shy away from difficult and taboo topics!**

Whilst it may feel so much safer to bury your head in the sand, the truth is that the avoidance of difficult conversation topics can be extremely damaging to our mental health and wellbeing. **I strongly believe that our refusal to talk about supposedly 'taboo' topics is causing us a lot more harm than good.**

Refusing to talk about death, for example, does not mean that death no longer exists. Similarly, refusing to talk about depression does not make it just go away – it just means that more people suffer from this crippling mental health condition in silence. It could not be clearer: **Starting difficult conversations may be difficult, but it will undoubtedly save and transform lives.** Talking about tough topics such as depression and death is one of the bravest things that any of us can ever do.

It is not acceptable for us to shy away from talking about society's biggest taboos. We need to tackle them head-on, no matter how awkward or uncomfortable this may make us feel.

BE BRAVE ENOUGH TO START A CONVERSATION THAT MATTERS.

Stop letting fear, stigma, and shame holding us back from talking about the conversational topics that really matter.

We cannot shy away from difficult or controversial conversation topics because we are scared about having these discussions.

I understand why you might feel worried about saying the wrong thing and I why you might feel anxious not wanting to cause upset or offence. **But saying something – anything – is always better than remaining silent.**

We cannot avoid these important issues, no matter how uncomfortable or scared they make us feel. **We must have these frank conversations with the people that matter in our lives. If we do not, we all continue to suffer in silence.**

A problem shared, as they always say, is a problem halved. When we talk about our biggest fears, **we find ourselves feeling more empowered than we have ever felt before.** We realise that silence is suffocating and that **conversation is cathartic! Starting difficult conversations and daring to talk about our fears, worries and vulnerabilities is the solution to all of our suffering!**

When starting a difficult conversation, it is only natural to feel a certain amount of anxiety. You are, after all, taking a plunge into depths potentially unknown. Who knows what we might find ourselves sharing? Who knows what uncomfortable truths we might find ourselves hearing?

When trying to start a difficult conversation, it is important to realise that there is never a 'wrong' thing to say. As long as you approach the conversation with *good intentions* and a real attitude of openness, then you have absolutely nothing to fear whatsoever!

The first thing you need to do is pick the right moment. You might ask someone if they have a spare hour for a cup of tea and a chat, for example. Don't feel anxious about picking the right moment, but just be mindful of picking an appropriate context. For example, I don't advise picking a nightclub dancefloor as the place to strike up conversation about God or death! You don't need to make it overly formal – it's not a business meeting where you need to hire a board room and get dressed up!

Simply pick a calm moment in the day when you can invest your full attention in the conversation. You don't want to be distracted and you don't want to be worried about other people getting involved.

Pick an appropriate time and context where you won't be dis-

turbed – but **don't overthink it and work yourself up about it!**
It's important to strike up conversation whilst that iron is hot!

Once you've seized your moment – and have a good cup of tea,
or something stronger, in hand – it's time to start talking.

Again, **remind yourself that this does not have to be a big deal
– you are just having a chat about something you think that it
is important to discuss.**

The best way to start a difficult conversation isn't actually
with words – **the best way to it start is by making sure that
you have got the right attitude.**

That's because **the secret to successfully starting a difficult
conversation is maintaining a mental attitude of openness.**

We must approach any taboo topic with a real attitude of
openness, **where we can put our fears and preconceptions to
one side.**

Our body language must signal this openness – make yourself
appear as 'open' as possible, including making eye contact and
uncrossing your arms.

Once you have signalled openness through your body language, **you have then just got to take that plunge and get down
to business!** Stop working yourself up and stop overthinking
it in your head – **simply calmly and confidently start the conversation!** *Yes, it really is that simple!*

You might find that **using a current affairs link** helps start the
discussion – for example, if there has been a high profile death
covered in the news, you might begin a conversation about
the arrangements for after your own death (e.g. your funeral
or the details of your will) by talking about this.

Express your sadness about the news, before opening the discussion up to the wider subject of mortality.

You could, for example, ask your conversational partner about their own thoughts on the prospect of 'life after death'.

Or, if you wanted to open up to someone about your sexual orientation, you could talk about a celebrity coming out as gay in a television interview.

After making a comment about how brave or inspiring they are, you could then seamlessly shift the discussion to the topic of your own sexual orientation.

Whether you use these 'current affairs links' or not, always remember this: **As long as you keep an attitude of openness and make a commitment to absolute honesty in your discussion, you have nothing to worry about whatsoever!**

You have got to ask yourself this: **what is the worst thing that can actually happen here?** Remember that **whatever happens in life, you can handle it!**

I mean what is actually the worst-case scenario - that the other person might not be willing to listen to what you have to say or might not be prepared to have this conversation with you now? It's hardly the end of the world, is it!

Whatever happens, be proud of the fact that you found the confidence to start this tricky discussion – you have shown incredible courage and done something truly extraordinary!

If the conversation *doesn't* end up going as well as you'd hoped it would, don't take it personally! Some people do just take longer to come around and face their fears.

Just because somebody doesn't want to talk to you about a difficult topic - such as death or their sexual orientation - right now, that doesn't mean that they never will.

What you need to know is this: **When you start difficult conversations about deeply taboo topics, you are sowing the seeds for societal transformation.** In raising these challenging subject areas, you are actively helping the *whole* of society to become a more enlightened and open place.

When you have these important types of radically honest and open conversation, you quite literally change lives... starting with your very own.

Opening up, starting a difficult conversation and daring to be vulnerable is the most powerful and empowering thing you can ever do.

So what are you waiting for? **Stop letting your fears hold you back from starting those difficult discussions on these so-called 'taboo' topics.**

Approach these conversations with courage and openness, remembering that you have nothing to fear whatsoever.

<u>Get comfortable with feeling vulnerable and know that it is okay to say to someone that you're not actually okay.</u>

Share your fears, share your inner feelings and watch how daring to be so open transforms your entire experience of life.

When we engage with tough topics, we gain power over them. They no longer fill us with dread or fear, and we are no longer shamed into silence. **All that it takes is just one conversation, and all that it requires is an attitude of openness.**

Let's get confident about opening up, daring to be vulnerable, and starting those difficult discussions. Let's free ourselves from our conversational fears and smash to pieces our discussion topic taboos – my dear reader, it is time to talk!

You've got this, so don't you dare fear those difficult conversations!

Remember that talking saves and changes lives! *By starting a difficult conversation, you have so much to gain and absolutely nothing to lose.*

Saying something is always so much better than suffering in silence...

48. CELEBRATE LIFE'S SIMPLE PLEASURES

"Simplicity is the ultimate sophistication" (Leonardo Da Vinci)

There is a real belief in our modern society that happiness is a case of 'the bigger the better' (now don't be cheeky about that one!) Our consumerist culture feeds us this narrative that the only way to be happy is to have the biggest car, the biggest house and the biggest bank balance.

Happiness, we are told, is achieved through extravagant demonstrations of power and wealth. How could you possibly be happy if you're not a millionaire with a super-yacht and private island in the sun?

This is all a complete fabrication. Businesses want to fool us into thinking that the only way to find happiness is if we buy it from them.

Capitalism has turned happiness into a commodity that can be bought and sold, and as a result money has become the new measure of whether someone is happy in life.

Businesses today make billions of pounds from commercialising and commodifying happiness. As a result, every business marketing strategy is focused on promoting a message that

'YOU CAN BUY YOUR WAY TO HAPPINESS!' and that 'BY FILL-ING YOUR HOUSE WITH EXPENSIVE THINGS, YOU WILL BE ABLE TO FILL YOUR SOUL!'

The reality is, of course, that constantly consuming more will never make you happy.

That's because businesses make it their mission to ensure you are never satisfied or fulfilled – it is in their interest that you are never content, because then you will keep going back to buy more and more.

In a capitalist system dependent on constant spending and consumption, it is essential that no-one ever feels they have enough…the economy would collapse if we no longer wanted to spend, spend and spend!

Now whilst there is nothing wrong with spending all your money on buying the latest products being promoted, it is so important for us to realise that an addiction to consumption will NEVER MAKE YOU HAPPY.

In fact, all it will do is leave you feeling more unfulfilled and empty than ever before!

The truth is this: **it's not just your pockets that these busi-nesses are leaving empty…it is your soul as well!**

If we want to experience real happiness in our lives, we need to start realising that it is the smallest of pleasures that bring us the greatest amount of joy.

Happiness is all about living with a sense of purpose and tak-ing pleasure in the simple things in life. Happiness is a good cup of tea, a good book or a long walk at sunset with your soulmate.

That's right, happiness is found through the enjoyment of life's most simple pleasures!

Instead of being bought by super-yachts and smartphones, happiness is found through appreciating life's simplest pleasures!

Here are a couple of my all-time favourite 'simple pleasures' -

- A good cup of tea or coffee
- Relaxing with the newspaper or a favourite magazine
- Reading a good book
- Catching up on your favourite TV show
- Enjoying your favourite meal
- Watching the sunrise or sunset
- A long walk in beautiful surroundings
- A night in with your partner
- Taking a long and relaxing bath
- A hot chocolate by the fire
- An early night after a very long day
- An insightful and invigorating conversation
- A day on the beach
- Classical music and meditation
- Making someone's day with a smile
- Watching a Christmas movie

These simple pleasures cost you very little – or absolutely nothing at all – and yet are capable of bringing you so much happiness and joy.

And so, if we want to find genuine happiness and fulfilment as human beings, we need learn how to to slow down and start enjoying the simple pleasures in life. This is the (very simple) secret to living a genuinely good life!

So what simple pleasures will you make a real effort to appreciate and enjoy in your life today?

Fill your moment with little moments of bliss, and start living your very best life!

49. TRY A NEW PERSPECTIVE!

"Everything we hear is an opinion, not a fact. Everything we see is a perspective, not the truth" (Marcus Aurelius)

How easily do you get caught up in your thoughts? How often do you let your mind run away with itself? How much time do you spend overthinking things that have happened or endlessly worrying about what might potentially happen one day in the future?

We spend so much of lives lost in our own heads, where we construct different narratives and make different interpretations about what is going on in the world.

"There is nothing either good or bad but thinking makes it so". These are the words of William Shakespeare, the 16th-century playwright taught to English Literature students across the globe.

As human beings, we have a tendency to automatically believe our thoughts and assume that they are correct.

We simply take at 'face value' the interpretations that our minds make. If something makes us angry, for example, we don't ask 'why' it is making us feel this way but simply allow the emotion to overwhelm us.

Or if we are feeling scared about something, we don't ask whether our fear is rational or not – we just let the emotion take over . When we do this, we are forgetting that our thoughts and beliefs are not always rational.

As a result, we often fail to identify potentially dangerous biases and errors in our thinking.

These errors can cause enormous amounts of distress and suffering in our lives.

It is therefore **vitally important that we get serious about monitoring our minds and making it our mission to regularly review the rationality of our thoughts.**

John Stuart Mill wrote back in the 18th century that we must all be vigilant to avoid the **"deep slumber of a decided opinion".**

When we assume that we know everything about a subject and that what we believe is 100% correct, we are making a grave mistake! We are achieving extraordinarily high new levels of ignorance, and let me tell you something right now - **this ignorance is absolutely not bliss! Instead, ignorance is nothing but an absolute recipe for disaster!**

Living in ignorance about the true origins of our beliefs means we are liable to start blindly believing irrational thoughts that are just not true!

For example, you might assume that you know exactly what somebody thinks about you. Or you might assume that you definitely will not get that dream job you've applied for.

When we just accept our thoughts and beliefs without subjecting them to evaluation or review, we are committing a the

most shocking act of self-sabotage.

We are unnecessarily limiting ourselves and writing ourselves off.

We are jumping to conclusions and living our lives based on biases in our thinking that are supported by absolutely no evidence whatsoever!

This is why it is so important to start challenging and critiquing your perceptions.

Try not take your thoughts at face value – accept that they are there but don't blindly believe that they are correct.

Whenever you find yourself dealing with a difficult thought or feeling, it is essential that you take some time to 'get some perspective'.

Let me give you an 'out-of-this-world' example that demonstrates the importance of getting some perspective!

The **'overview effect'** refers to the cognitive shift in awareness reported by many astronauts when they first go into space.

It refers to the changes in thinking they experience as a result of seeing earth from the vantage point of space.

For the first time, and with their very own eyes, these astronauts see the earth as this tiny little fragile ball against the backdrop of our overwhelmingly massive universe.

Michael Collins, an astronaut on the Apollo 11 spaceflight, put it like this: **"The thing that really surprised me was that it [the Earth] projected an air of fragility…I had a feeling it's tiny, it's shiny, it's beautiful, it's home and it's fragile"**.

Apollo 14 astronaut Edgar Mitchell explains: **"You develop an instant global consciousness, a people orientation, an intense dissatisfaction with the state of the world, and a com-**

pulsion to do something about it. From out there on the moon, international politics look so petty".

Both these astronauts, and many others, had their perspectives on earthly life totally transformed by their experiences in space.

As a result of taking a 'birds-eye' view of our planet, they saw life on earth in a totally different light. Looking down on the tiny planet that they called home, they were amazed and overwhelmed by what they saw.

This new perspective radically altered the way in which they would think about life on earth forever. Everything about their earthly lives had suddenly just been put into a whole new perspective.

It's not just astronauts who can enjoy the benefits of the 'overview effect'. In our own lives, we can all reap the rewards of 'getting some perspective' and taking a 'birds-eye view' on our lives!

To do this, we need to start stepping outside of our everyday experiences and to start getting better at seeing the 'bigger picture' in our lives.

We need to start putting our problems into perspective and asking ourselves – **what is really going on here? Do I really need to lose sleep over this situation? Will all of this not be forgotten about within 6 weeks?**

Ask yourself this: Is there evidence for what I am thinking about this situation, or is my mind getting carried away with itself? Is how I am feeling about this situation based on genuine facts or my irrational fears?

I like to think of it like this: Imagine that you are a scientist in the science lab of life.

You've got your lab coat on and your thoughts are not inside your head but instead in front of you in a test tube. Take some time to really test and interrogate them – observe them and evaluate them!

Do they contain the truth? Or are they being unduly influenced by your fears and biases in your thinking?

Are you making a complete mountain out of a tiny molehill, and unnecessarily getting yourself worked up about something that should not even be an issue?

As Robert Holden once said, **"One new perception, one fresh thought, one act of surrender, one leap of faith ... can change your life forever"**.

So strive to see the bigger picture.

Think like one of those astronauts looking down from space and taking in the 'birds eye' view.

Put your earthly problems into perspective and start living with greater clarity and calm than ever before!

50. DON'T TAKE YOURSELF TOO SERIOUSLY

"Laughter is, and will always be, the best form of therapy" (Popular Aphorism)

Too many of us take ourselves far too seriously. We approach trivial issues like they are matters of life and death, and endlessly worry about things that, in reality, really do not matter.

We are so anxious about how we look to other people that we are terrified of letting our hair down, kicking off our shoes, and having a good bit of fun!

I believe that in order to live your best life, a good sense of humour is absolutely essential! A good sense of humour not only makes you more likable to other people, but it also means that you will like YOURSELF more!

When you have a good sense of humour, you are no longer anxious about being laughed at or worried about making a fool of yourself. When you start living a life filled with laughter, your paralysing fear of being embarrassed or making mistakes is extinguished overnight.

I strongly believe that life presents us with two very clear choices: we can either choose to take everything seriously and walk around on eggshells, or we can decide to live with

a sense of humour and laugh our way through each and every day!

In order to live a truly happy life, it is essential that you top worrying about being embarrassed or getting ridiculed!

Whenever you're doing something that really scares you or takes you well outside of your comfort zone, always think to yourself: **if things don't work out the way I have planned, at least I'll have a funny story to tell at my next dinner party!**

I like to imagine that my life is a reality TV show or one of the 'Carry On' films – it is the times when things go wrong that make for the most entertaining viewing!

I turn every embarrassment and unnecessary drama in my life into a TikTok video…and as a result my account typically gets over 15 million views a month! I am able to turn my anxiety and adversity into comedy-gold entertainment that brings a smile to faces across the nation!

Life would be very boring if everything went to plan…

Stop desperately desiring perfection and start living your life to the full instead!

Endlessly trying to 'keep up appearances' will lead to nothing but sadness, misery, and anxiety in your life. It is absolutely essential that we learn to let go, loosen up and laugh at ourselves!

At the end of the day, **there are always much worse things going on in the world than whatever it is that we are going through right now.**

So count your blessings, realise that whatever you're going through is really not that deep, and get on with your day!

As long as your alive, you have absolutely no excuse not to be laughing your way through each and every day!

People love someone who can entertain them, and **the most entertaining people are those who can make a joke - and take a joke - at their own expense. Strive to become secure enough in your own skin so that you can make a joke about your own misfortunes and crack a joke about the flaws in your personality.**

Don't be so sensitive and serious about everything – have a laugh and share a smile!

At the end of the day, nothing is really that deep. Whatever has gone wrong today will almost certainly be forgotten about by tomorrow.

Humour is an excellent strategy for defusing haters and putting them back in their box.

Of course, it is perfectly normal to feel hurt by what someone says about you, but I promise you that **the best way to defuse anyone causing you unhappiness is to hit back with humour!**

When you are confident enough to laugh at yourself and laugh off people's pathetic judgments and comments, **you send a very clear signal to the world that you are 100% secure in your own skin.**

Think about it: What is the one thing that haters, trolls, bullies and gossips want? A reaction!

You should therefore make it your mission to NOT give the the haters that dramatic and emotional reaction they are craving! Instead, turn their hate into humour and quite simply laugh it off!

Show them just how confident, self-accepting and strong you really are - show them how what they are saying is so pathetic that it is actually entertaining, rather than offending, you.

I really do believe that if someone says anything rude or derogatory about you, it does you no favours to be sensitive and get upset about it.

You need to show the haters that you are not going to let them get you down!

So instead of letting them get you down, turn their spiteful comments into an opportunity for comedy and a good giggle!

Crack a joke about it, undermine them using humour, and show them very clearly that their words will not get you down!

Remember: You should never be ashamed of any part of who you are. You should never be embarrassed about making mistakes or showing a bit of emotion. You deserve to live a truly authentic life at all times. **In order to do this, <u>you have to stop taking yourself so seriously.</u>**

If you care too much about how you look or what other people are going to think, you turn your life into an inescapable cesspit of worry and anxiety.

You feel that everyone has their eyes on you and that they're almost waiting for you to fail. **This is a toxic mindset!**

The best way to conquer this very negative mindset is with a good sense of humour!

You start living your very best life when you discover your ability to laugh at yourself!

Always find time to have a good giggle about all of your successes and failures in life!

Being able to poke fun at yourself is extremely good for your soul.

Think of it like this: **every drama you experience today is a good dinner party anecdote for tomorrow!** If you fell over in front of a hundred people this morning, you can have a good laugh about it over a glass of wine at tonight.

If you forgot your words mid-speech at an important conference last month, turn that trauma into an entertaining talking point on your next cocktail date!

Show the world that you can have a good laugh at your own expense, and you will never be short of friends!

We all make mistakes and we all embarrass ourselves from time to time – **the trick is to learn from those mistakes and confidently laugh them off.** Stop caring about whether you have made a fool of yourself and start enjoying every single day of your life instead!

So stop taking yourself too seriously! I hate to break it to you, but nobody actually cares about what you did wrong!

Nobody is actually that interested in the fact you made a mistake or that you embarrassed yourself at that function! Nobody is actually keeping notes on how many times you've made a mistake!

Everyone is too busy focusing on their own problems to care one tiny bit!

People are like goldfish when it comes to remembering other people's misfortunes - they've forgotten about what happened within an hour!

Laugh your way through life and you will enjoy it so much more! Life is far too short to taken too seriously!

As long as you are alive, you are capable of having a good laugh – and that is exactly what you should keep choosing to do!

Choose to look on the bright side and stop treating trivial

issues like they are matters of life and death! *Stop taking your-self so seriously, and start living your life to the full instead!*

51. ENJOY EVERYTHING IN MODERATION

"A little bit of what you fancy does you good" (my Granny – Queen Wendy)

The secret to enjoying a happy and balanced life is enjoying everything in moderation. This really is a golden rule for living – a little bit of what you fancy does you good…but too much of anything is never good!

A happy life should resemble a pie chart (please bear with me, I promise it will start to make sense very soon…)

Take a moment to imagine your life as if it were a pie chart.

Imagine that the pie chart represents your life as a whole and that the different 'slices' of the pie represent the different areas of your life.

Fill your pie chart with all of the different areas of your life – work, dating, sex life, eating out, the gym, sleep, gardening. **Is there any area of your life that seems to take over your pie chart?** For example, is your life 90% work and then 10%

everything else? **We should strive to create lives that resemble well-balanced pie charts.**

In order to feel fulfilled and become the best versions of ourselves, we need a healthy balance of different interests.

At certain times in your life, I have no doubt that particular interests will inevitably dominate your days and take up a disproportionate amount of your time, but as a general rule try to establish that well-balanced pie chart in your life.

This means making sure you have time in your life for everything that keeps you happy and healthy as a human being – strive to enjoy everything in moderation!

This idea that you should try to enjoy 'everything in moderation' can be traced back over 2,500 years to the writing of Aristotle, a key philosopher who has featured countless times in this book!

Aristotle proposed that in life, we should strive to at

tain a so-called 'golden mean'. The golden mean is the desirable middle point between two extremes – excess (too much) and deficiency (too little).

Aristotle applied this to the cultivation of moral virtues such as courage. Courage is the 'golden mean' between two extremes. If taken to the excess, courage becomes recklessness. If totally deficient (absent), courage becomes cowardice. The virtue we refer to as 'Courage' is therefore seen as such a noble and desirable moral virtue because it perfectly achieves a golden mean between two extremes.

The concept of the 'golden mean' shouldn't just be applied to the practice and cultivation of virtues - we should strive to achieve the 'golden mean' in every single area of our lives. What does this mean?

It means living a life of BALANCE! Your life should represent that well-balanced pie chart (I hope the analogy is making a lot more sense now!) **with your life made up of a very healthy**

selection of different interests and activities.

As they say, **variety is the spice of life!** To flourish as an individual, **you need to live a life of balance and diversity**! It is very simple - **a happy life is a balanced life**.

As my granny always tells me, 'a little bit of what you fancy does you good'.

It's important to make room for all of your interests and needs in daily life!

Don't deprive yourself of the things you love and need, but equally don't take anything to the excess.

Strive to achieve that perfect golden mean! Instead of putting all of your eggs in one basket, seek to achieve that healthy balance of work, rest and play.

If you start depriving yourself of essential human needs - for example, you don't make time in your day to relax or to cultivate meaningful relationships - you'll end up paying the price. **You need to make sure your life represents a well-balanced pie chart!**

Make sure there's room for all your interests and basic human needs!

You've only got 24 hours in your day, so it's your job to make sure you spend them wisely.

We've got to strike that healthy balance which will allow us to thrive through life!

You need to remember that a little bit of what you fancy does you good - but be careful not to take things to the absolute extreme!

And so you go through life, try to maintain the well-balanced pie chart as much as you possibly can.

At all times, try to remember that life is all about balance. This really is the secret to thriving as a happy and healthy human being!

*Also, make sure you remember that **balance is a fine art - don't beat yourself up about the fact that you don't always manage to keep that balance perfect!***

<u>**The most important thing is that you are doing your best to maintain this 'golden mean' in all of the things that you do**</u>.

Aspire to find that healthy balance and consequently enjoy a truly happy, fulfilling and enriching life.

Remember – **there's room in your day for ALL of your interests and needs!**

Ultimately, success in life all comes down to intelligently managing your personal life pie chart!

And **the secret to achieving this is some good planning, organisation, and always keeping in mind that 'a little bit of what you fancy does you good!'**

52. CELEBRATE EVERY ACHIEVEMENT

"The highest reward for a man's toll is not what he gets for it but what he becomes by it" (John Ruskin)

Your success in life is for you and nobody else. You should be striving to achieve in life not in order to impress other people but, as I have argued throughout this book, in order to fulfil your potential and become the best version of yourself.

You should be aspiring to 'live your best life' not in order to gain the approval of others but so that you yourself feel deeply proud and empowered in your own skin.

You should strive to do well in this world not because you crave validation from other people but in order to fulfil your potential as a human being.

This is why you should start spending time reflecting on and celebrating all of your personal successes and achievements.

In life, we work so hard to achieve our dreams and do our best, yet it can so often feel like we are never doing enough.

There is always someone with more than us, in the same way that there is always someone with less than us. It can feel like we are stuck on a hamster wheel, continuously chasing success but feeling like we're actually just going round and round in circles.

As I always say, **the only person you should compete with is who you were yesterday.**

Life is not about becoming the winner of every single race but about becoming the very best version of yourself.

This is why it is essential for you to take time to celebrate your achievements and chart your journey of self-growth so far.

Taking this time to reflect on how far you have come and celebrate all of the things you have achieved so far is one of the most life-affirming and mood-boosting things that you can ever do!

Get serious about having gratitude for your journey!

 What I want you to do is grab your pen and paper – or even the notes section on your phone – and write down a list of 5 of your biggest achievements in life so far. Bullet point them down on your sheet and write a little bit about what those achievements mean to you.

In case you're looking for a bit of inspiration, here's mine:

•   **Overcoming the eating disorder anorexia after being hospitalised and told that I was going to die.** I am proud of taking back control of my life and making the most of the amazing therapy I was able to receive. This experience transformed my whole attitude and approach towards life. I now see life as the most precious of gifts which should be lived to the full. I am proud of the hard work that I have put in to get to where I am today. I am proud to have worked so hard at transforming my life from a place of self-hatred and starvation to an existence filled with gratitude, enjoyment and optimism.

•   **Getting a job aged 17 at a local 5* hotel.** I was doing 'meet & greet' on reception and getting this job was the best thing I ever did in my life. It opened so many doors and gave me the most incredible confidence for working with people. I loved every single second of my time in this job and believe it genuinely made me who I am today – the people skills I learnt and the experiences I had will never be forgotten in my whole lifetime. I am proud of going out and getting this job, and proud of throwing myself into it with so much enthusiasm.

•   **Moving to London and studying religion, philosophy & ethics at King's College, London.** Oh I put blood, sweat and tears into getting a place on this course, let me tell you now! I'd had my heart set on studying and living in London for quite literally YEARS, and I am so proud to have finally turned this dream into my reality. I feel so proud to think that I managed to conquer the capital and have made London a place that genuinely feels like home! When I'm out and about in London, I now know exactly where I'm going (well, most of the time) and I like to think that I have become quite the expert at navigating the London Underground...even at rush hour! I am so proud to have taken to London like a duck to water – I genuinely have to pinch myself as I think about how my commute to university involves walking through Trafalgar Square and past Buckingham Palace! I am so proud of the confidence I have found, the people I have met and the fact that London really does now feel like a home. I love to sit back and reflect on my journey from living in a small-town to taking London by storm!

•   **Spending a year working at Europe's biggest LGBT nightclub** – One of the things I never thought in a million years I would do! This was – okay I know I keep saying this – the most incredible experience of my life. This was another job that helped my confidence to soar through the roof, as well as teaching me incredible life lessons I will cherish for the rest of my life! On my very first weekend in London, I went out and got this job – that same weekend I was working my first 10pm – 5am shift serving 2,000 people on the front reception desk of the club. It was just incredible and, despite the fact I used to go to bed at 9.30pm every night, the best experience of my life. To get myself into the very epicentre of the London gay scene and have this incredible time – as well as earning money from it – makes me so proud and so happy. I have so much gratitude for this incredible experience that made me who I am – and again I'm proud to have gone and got this for myself, and to have totally thrown myself into making a success of it. The biggest blessing of my life so far, however crazy that may seem!

• **Fully accepting who I am** – none of these achievements would have been possible without perhaps the most important achievement of my life so far: accepting my sexuality and finding confidence in my identity. It breaks my heart when I see how many people go through life ashamed of their sexual orientation and terrified of people's opinions of them. I am so immensely proud that I was able to educate myself about homosexuality, which empowered me to accept being gay, safe in the knowledge it was natural, normal, and actually morally acceptable. My study of religion and philosophy confirmed for me that there was nothing wrong with being homosexual and allowed me to realise that all homophobia is totally groundless. This was the most empowering realisation of my life – I was able to become 110% secure in my own mind that my sexuality was nothing to be ashamed of, and so I had absolute confidence in being true to myself in the world. This is the kind of impenetrable self-certainty and self-confidence that money can't buy! Getting to this place of total confidence and empowerment has set me up for life, and it makes me so proud to be able to live my truth and know my worth every single day of my life. This, in my opinion, is what life is all about.

Reading those back, I feel an immense sense of pride about what I've achieved. Looking back on these achievements reminds me of what I passionately believe about life: **Your existence on this planet is all about overcoming your fears, stepping outside of your comfort zone, and becoming the very best version of yourself!**

We must keep taking on new challenges that enlarge our lives and enrich us as human beings.

Let your past victories and achievements give you inspiration and motivation for the future!

Keep taking risks and keep putting yourself out there, because this will mean that your life continues to get bigger and bigger.

When it comes to reflecting on your own achievements, I always worry about coming across as self-obsessed.

But here's the thing: **there is nothing wrong with celebrating what you have achieved in your life!**

We need to be loud and proud about our achievements in life!!

Be immensely proud of who you are, what you've achieved and of what you have overcome! You have worked SO hard to get to where you are today - so celebrate your successes and sing your own praises from the rooftops!

Crack open that prosecco and let off a confetti canon or two! You're the one who has put in so much hard work to get here, and so you deserve to give yourself a good pat on the back!

It is your duty – to yourself – to be proud of what you have achieved so far in your life!

We all seem to dwell far too much on the times when we have supposedly embarrassed ourselves or got things wrong.

Well, if we can spend all of this time dwelling on the times when things have gone wrong, then I think that we should also find the time to celebrate the times when things actually went well!

Be proud of what you have achieved so far and know that this is just the beginning of a lifetime of success! Celebrate your achievements and be proud of the person you are today!

You are doing an amazing job on this journey through life, and there is plenty more success to come...

53. WHATEVER HAPPENS IN LIFE, YOU CAN HANDLE IT

"A comfort zone is a beautiful place, but nothing ever grows there" (Popular Aphorism)

So here we are, we've made it to the end of this journey together! And, if I may say so, what a journey it has been! I say that this is the end, but really this is just the beginning! Oh yes, this is where the fun begins, because **it's now time to start putting all these ideas into practice!**

It's time to head out and face the world with all that confidence, authenticity and resilience we have been talking about! As Seneca once said, **'every new beginning comes from some other beginning's end'.** *The end of this book means the beginning of your brand new life!*

It's time to start actively living your best life and put into practice all that hard work and perseverance we have been talking about! **The question is this: are you ready to embark on the journey of a lifetime?**

Here's what I want you to know: **Whatever you are going**

through in life right now, know that you can handle it. No matter how tough times seem, remember that there is a light at the end of this tunnel.

With hope, faith and love absolutely anything is possible. At all times, always remember to be guided by your core values and anchored in your strong moral principles. At all times, allow your life to be illuminated by the beacon of light that is love. Remember the words of St Paul – "love always protects, always trusts, always hopes and always perseveres". Most importantly, remember that **love never fails.**

Know that you deserve to live a truly happy and fulfilling existence.

Never apologise for being who you authentically are, and never lower your vibration in an attempt to please negative or judgmental people.

Instead of worrying about what other people think, become passionate about becoming the very best version of yourself.

Stop letting your fear of rejection and failure hold you back from living your life to the full. You are stronger than you think!

Always remember - **you are enough and your life has infinite worth.** Stop being a prisoner to perfectionism; - realise that you do not have to get every single thing right on every single day of your life!

Allow yourself to make mistakes and, most importantly, allow yourself to learn from them.

As I always say, **you grow through what you go through! Embrace failure and transform every obstacle into another op-**

portunity to grow.

There is nothing to fear about getting things wrong – the more mistakes we make, the wiser we become!

In the words of JK Rowling, *'It is impossible to live without failing at something, unless you live so cautiously that you might as well have not lived at all'.*

Make it your mission to form as many meaningful and genuine relationships as you can. Fill your life with authentic friendships built on those essential 'feelings of affection', and build for yourself a loving family.

Never tire of showing love, kindness, and compassion to every single person that you meet.

Realise that you will find true purpose in life when you start connecting with these three things: the present moment, other people and with who you authentically are.

Seize every opportunity to live a fearlessly authentic life and to make a positive difference in this world that we are so blessed to live in. Strive to become a beacon of light who brings love, hope, and happiness into the lives of every single person that you meet.

Make it your mission to turn everything you touch into gold. Approach every stranger as if they were just a friend that you haven't had the good fortune of meeting yet.

Most importantly, remember that whatever happens in life,

you can handle it. No matter what happens or what anybody says, hold your head up high.

Stand up for yourself and at all times know your worth. Never suffer through anything in silence – remember that asking for help is always an act of strength and is never a sign of weakness.

Tirelessly work hard at turning all of your dreams into your brand new reality. **Keep fulfilment as your number one priority in life!** Remember, you were not born just to survive each day but to thrive through every single moment! **Embrace change and seize the day, remembering that you never know which day could be your last.**

With that in mind, make sure that you **never miss an opportunity to spread love, build relationships, empower others, and grow as a human being.**

Never waste a moment worrying about what could potentially go wrong or regretting what has happened in your past.

Every moment is a brand-new opportunity to live your best life and to become the best version of yourself. Remember what Kierkegaard says - life is not a problem to be solved but a reality to be experienced.

May you fully grab life with both hands and make the most of every single opportunity the universe offers you. Stop doubting your worth and stop imposing limitations on your potential.

This is your one and only life – may you live every single second of it to the absolute full.

Stop caring what other people think and stop letting worries about what could happen hold you back.

You must be totally confident and utterly fearless in living your best life.

Dare to be authentic and dare to fulfil your potential as a human being.

This is your time to shine and to live a life guided by the eternal light of love.

When your life becomes illuminated by love, absolutely anything becomes possible.

Every obstacle can be transformed into an opportunity, and every challenge becomes a catalyst for self-growth and personal development.

In the words of Charles Marcus:

"Whatever challenges you are facing, you can overcome them. The only limitations are those you impose on yourself. Believe in yourself, find your inner strength, have courage, be 100 percent committed. Take full responsibility for your life, surround yourself with positive, supportive people, and dream big, big dreams. They really do come true".

From the very bottom of my heart, I wish you all of the authenticity, confidence and resilience in the world.

You deserve nothing less than a truly happy and deeply fulfilling life.

May you dare to be fearlessly authentic.

May you dare to become the author of your next chapter.

May you dare to live your best life.

AFTERWORD

"Keep your face always toward the sunshine – and shadows will fall behind you" (Walt Whitman)

Well here we are; we've made it to the end of this exploration of authenticity, confidence & resilience. Thank you so much for joining me.

But really, of course, this is only just the beginning of the journey! That's right, the hard work starts right here! It's now your time to shine! It's time to face your fears, tackle your insecurities and commit to living your very best life as the best version of yourself.

It's time to get out there and grab every opportunity life goes you with both hands - it's time to turn those dreams into your reality!

Let me just say this: I believe in you! Even if you're not convinced you've got what it takes to put yourself out there and live fearlessly, let me tell you right now - you've got this!

The only thing holding you back from living your best life is your self-defeating belief that you can't! Remember at all times that whatever happens, you can handle it. Keep stepping outside of your comfort zone. Keep daring to live life as your very best and most authentic self.

Let me just share with you these inspiring words from F. Scott Fitzgerald:

"For what it's worth: it's never too late to be whoever you want to be. I hope you live a life you're proud of, and if you find that you're not, I hope you have the strength to start over".

So what are you waiting for? We know that you deserve to be happy, that you deserve to fulfil your potential and to become the very best version of yourself. You deserve to get out there and live your best life. So let's get to work!

Thank you for reading, and thank you for committing to live an authentic, fulfiling and - most importantly - happy life.

By fearlessly living as your authentic self, you are inspiring thousands of other people to do the same. Show anyone currently going through a dark time that there is light at the end of the tunnel. Become a beacon of light and a symbol of hope for all of those currently struggling in silence. Aspire to Inspire every single person that you meet.

Know your worth and be unashamedly authentic in the way that you live your life. Fearlessly turn all of your biggest dreams into your brand-new reality.

Remember that you only ever get what you put with in life , and remember that you only deserve the very best in life.

This is your one life – so make sure that you live every single second of it to the absolute full.

You are the master of your own destiny and the author of your next chapter. Your future starts right here. Only one question remains - ***Are you ready to thrive?***

Until next time, take care of yourself. Now get out there and ***LIVE YOUR BEST LIFE!***

With all of my love,

Ben Xx

BEN WARDLE | **benwardle.org**

June 2020.

Keep up to date with my
blog posts & upcoming
book releases at -

benwardle.org

Printed in Great Britain
by Amazon

43885716R00194